KNOWING, COLLECTING AND RESTORING EARLY AMERICAN FURNITURE

BY HENRY HAMMOND TAYLOR

WITH A FOREWORD BY
HOMER EATON KEYES
EDITOR OF *ANTIQUES*

59 ILLUSTRATIONS AND
22 LINE DRAWINGS

D1377337

DISCARDED

NEW HANOVER COUNTY
PUBLIC LIBRARY
201 CHESTNUT STREET
WILMINGTON, NC 28401

DISCARDED

PUBLIC LIBRARY

DEDICATED WITH DEEPEST GRATITUDE TO THAT ONE
FROM WHOM FIRST CAME MY INTEREST IN
THE FURNITURE AND POSSESSIONS OF
EARLY AMERICA

FOREWORD

M Y FIRST encounter with the problems involved in the refinishing of antique furniture occurred many years ago and impressed me deeply. A friend of mine, while somewhat overzealously engaged in scraping a venerable mahogany table top with a fragment of broken glass, seriously lacerated his hand. At the gory moment I felt that he had suffered a serious accident. Subsequently, I came to realize that the damage which he had sustained was insignificant in comparison with the ruin which he had inflicted upon the table. Time cures most human wounds; but naught avails to heal the mangled surface of a time-mellowed piece of furniture.

That lesson far too many American buyers of antiques have yet to learn. They have reached the point of cherishing the *idea* of age in their possessions, but have failed to attain full appreciation of the charm and value of its *aspect*. In consequence, they are prone to subject their early furniture to a course of scraping, sometimes of planing, to remove from it every vestige of stain and every remnant of honorable scar —all, indeed, of those outward and visible evidences of genuineness which are the precious endowment bestowed by the patient years upon comely old-time things.

And yet the opposite extreme, while less disastrous, is perhaps equally to be avoided. There is no merit in superficial deposits of dirt, and none in obvious and dangerous states of dilapidation and disrepair. American collectors, in general, like to use their old furniture for its originally designated purpose. When the fulfilment of that purpose is impaired, both prudence and good judgment counsel the application of remedial measures. There is, I know, a school of collectors who maintain that what time has sundered man

5

should not attempt to join. But their position seems hardly tenable. Things too far gone to respond to skilful treatment are certainly not worth having. Those which have measurably survived neglect and abuse deserve to be restored as nearly as possible to an estate normal to years of decent usage.

Briefly, in the restoring of antique furniture there is, or should be, an attainable golden mean, a sensible and temperate procedure, which, without countenancing misguided attempts at rejuvenation, will nevertheless accord to age its appropriate revelation of native vitality and inherent beauty. For those persons who would seek that mean and find it, I can think of no safer guidance—both philosophical and practical—than is discoverable in the pages of this book. For many years, the chief pastime of Henry Hammond Taylor, its author, has been the collecting and repairing of early American furniture. As a result, he is now possessed of an impressive assemblage of specimens, which he has himself dissected, analyzed, put together again, and, where necessary, restored and refinished. Some among his pieces have called for renewals in vital and conspicuous places. Yet, whether the required operation has been slight or extensive, it has, in every instance, been performed with such understanding, such sympathy—if I may use the term—and such rare combination of thoroughness and restraint as to afford no ground for criticism of things either left undone or carried to excess. And, not least important, the methods which he has employed are simple, straightforward, and quite within the comprehension of the average layman. His tools and apparatus are such as he has been able to house in a small workshop in his own home. Processes calling for more elaborate equipment he entrusts to professional hands. Judged by visible results, his methods are entirely adequate.

It was observation of these facts that led me to persuade Mr. Taylor to prepare for the magazine *Antiques* a series of brief articles on the restoration of furniture. Their publication met with sufficient success fully to justify their present expansion into book form. As now offered, their material has undergone essential amplification. An invaluable chapter on the philosophy of collecting has been added. Specific directions for the cleaning and refinishing of various kinds of wood have been made more specific, and have been clarified in matters of detail. The number of illustrations, all of them carefully prepared for this one treatise, has been greatly increased. The chapter on the proper choice of hardware is virtually new, and should remove many of the perplexities which beset amateur collector and professional cabinetmaker alike.

Perhaps relatively few of those who read this book will themselves attempt furniture refinishing on their own account. However lucid the given directions, they yet involve the expenditure of a good deal of time, labor, and patience, and a closer communion with unpleasant liquids than is calculated to rejoice fastidious noses or delicately nurtured hands. Nevertheless, knowledge of how such work should be performed, and of the results to be expected from it, is an essential part of every collector's equipment. Only with its aid may the owner of fine old items hope to safeguard them from mishandling by workmen brought up in the late tradition of flawless and highly polished wood surfaces, and of unnecessary substitutions of new parts for old.

Incidentally, too, the collecting neophyte who is at pains not only to absorb Mr. Taylor's direct comments but to realize their implications is likely to find himself, in the end, possessed of an unexpectedly fresh and penetrating critical vision. It is a fault of much writing on ways to detect fraudulent antiques that major emphasis is laid on the search for flaws, while training in the recognition of excellence is neglected. As a matter of fact, success in the collecting of antiques—as in all other of life's activities—lies not so much in avoiding the bad as in cleaving to the good. He who establishes an intelligent standard and rejects whatsoever falls below its level is in little danger of committing serious errors. In this book Mr. Taylor does not devote so much space to considering the specific earmarks of fraud as to steadfastly demonstrating the insignia of genuineness and quality; and he drives his points home not only with words, but with pictures so presented as to make them an inescapable part of the reader's visual memory. In thus enabling the beginning collector to acquire an affirmative rather than a negative point of view, he has performed an unusual and highly valuable service.

Of general works on period styles in furniture, and on the historic backgrounds of furniture, there are already a sufficient number to meet the normal requirements of both novitiate and veteran collector, and these are mentioned in the present volume. For some time, however, the need for a supplementary work of a semi-technical nature has been apparent. Thanks to the efforts of Mr. Taylor and his publishers that need seems now to be met. Various circumstances have pleasantly conspired to give to "Knowing, Collecting and Restoring Early American Furniture" a textual completeness and a fullness and aptness of pictorial illustration such as are seldom permitted to books intended primarily for popular consumption. They should insure its deserved occupancy of a permanent and honored place in the collector's library.

HOMER EATON KEYES

NEW YORK CITY
FEBRUARY, 1930

CONTENTS

ILLUSTRATIONS

LINE-CUTS IN TEXT

KNOWING, COLLECTING
AND RESTORING
EARLY AMERICAN
FURNITURE

Chapter 1
A WORD ON COLLECTING

THE interest in all sorts of early American articles both useful and decorative has tremendously increased throughout our land. It would seem that almost every cultured American home shelters at least one member who collects or at least has some knowledge of those things which were made and put to daily use by our ancestors. Museums which, not so long ago, gave scant attention to things American, now have fine collections properly classified and displayed. Local historical societies flourish, and, by means of frequent exhibits, bring to light fine examples of early American craftsmanship long hidden in seclusion. The popular magazines devote much space to articles on the collecting of American antiques.

We Americans have discovered that like other peoples we have a glorious past, and the discovery has stimulated us to investigate the lives, habits, and possessions of our ancestors. We absorb tales of our revolt against English rule, read eagerly about how the White House was furnished in 1830, and yearn to know precisely what things President Andrew Jackson was accustomed to eat for breakfast. Finding ourselves involved in a life of terrific speed and continued demands for high efficiency, we perhaps feel that some elements of the breadth and fineness, leisure and peace which our forebears enjoyed are no longer with us. As a hard-driven and much worried business man may, in enticing day-dreams, return in thought to boyhood days, so has America turned with a touch of vain regret to thoughts of early American men and women, their times, and the objects with which they surrounded themselves. And, while we may not

17

restore the past, we may gather together souvenirs of the olden days that lie so far away under a softening haze of happy illusion. So we have collectors of American furniture, pewter, glass, pottery, china, quilts, ironwork, lighting-fixtures, valentines, miniatures, prints, and whatnot else.

It is almost axiomatic that, sooner or later, all of our collectors will become collectors of furniture. Of course we often encounter families who, among their modern possessions, boast a few first-rate early American examples— "family pieces." Here, however, we are likely to find faint knowledge, strongly flavored with very inaccurate family tradition which insists that we regard with interest, and at least the simulation of reverence, late mahogany and Empire pieces which their owners optimistically assume to be a heritage from the Pilgrim century. But uninformed and accidental ownership of antiques entitles no one to membership in the great fraternity of collectors. For to be a collector we must collect, and we must, besides, exercise both knowledge and discretion in the process.

METHODS OF COLLECTING

Collecting may be undertaken in various ways. Some will buy only from reliable dealers. Others prefer to haunt junk and secondhand shops, small country auctions, or to travel from house to house in the country seeking bargains at their original source. Collecting from old country homes is most interesting, but it requires infinite patience, tact, and the ability to absorb vast quantities of sometimes not very interesting conversation. However, if occasionally such measures bring access to a real old-time attic crowded with ancient things, the recompense for much trouble may be considered adequate.

Collecting antiques from any and all sources is very closely allied to gambling, and, as a good gambler is supposed to lose with indifference or a smile, so should we meet our reverses and disappointments. And if our effort and our consequent experience should ever bring us to a position where our opinion is credited with some authority let us be a bit humble with it all.

Many of our most successful American collectors are, even with their great experience and knowledge, modest and open to new impressions. They do not give harsh and unasked criticism, correct every inaccurate statement of the enthusiastic beginner, or sneer at the possibly rather pathetic stock of some struggling dealer. They can politely view the Empire treasures of a newer collector without aspersions, always remembering that they themselves were once new at the game. They do not pretend, after one hasty glance in a bad light, immediately and infallibly to name the American woods used in a piece of furniture; nor do they broadcast the opinion that "dealers are a bunch of robbers," or "their prices are simply awful."

In justice we indeed may admit that the business road of the average dealer in antiques is not strewn with easy money. Every dealer works, and works hard, for any profit he may gain from his transactions. Knowing the rapidly increasing scarcity of antiques, I am in a constant state of wonderment that it is still possible to buy very good examples from dealers at such reasonable prices. I say this advisedly, for I am certain that, given a reasonable time, I could furnish a house with a very fair lot of antique pieces at an expenditure no greater than would be necessary for the purchase of good reproductions or modern furniture-store atrocities. And I could buy these antiques *from the dealers.* It is, however, only fair to admit that this home, when completed, would shelter few original butterfly tables or Philadelphia lowboys.

A friendly interest in our neighboring antique dealers, coupled with fair and honest treatment of them, particularly in the case of the smaller dealers, will be found a great help in collecting. But, if we wish both preference and the lowest prices, we should always pay cash. The collector who establishes a reputation for invariably paying "on the spot" gets the first look at the choice pieces after the dealer brings them home. An old Spanish proverb aptly covers this whole matter: "Will Pay is a fine bird, but Cash Down sings." Unless a purchase is covered by some special agreement or guarantee it should never be returned. Dealers soon learn to avoid the fickle and changeable collector who buys a piece one day and returns it the next with the excuse that "it didn't look well," or "it was too high," or "its legs were not quite enough cabriole."

I have many friends among the smaller dealers and "scouts," and have often been called by telephone at weird hours of the night to come and inspect some latest find. In city firehouses, the gallant firemen when they retire, place their trousers over a pair of rubber boots so that in the event of an alarm, they may spring from bed, jump into their boots and adjust the rest of their costume as they slide down a perpendicular brass rod running from the second to the first floor. My family has been kind enough to suggest that I should install the same system in my own home so that I may lose no time in answering these midnight antique alarms. But my family, I regret to confess, is, at times, given to gross exaggeration.

THE SATISFACTION OF ANTIQUES

A home completely furnished with a good collection of American antiques, acquired piece by piece from many sources, and in almost every conceivable way except theft, is, indeed, a delightful environment in which to live. Every piece will seem a friend, bringing to mind some interesting happening connected with its acquisition. In moments of leisure, and alone, the owner will often stroll through the

PLATE 1

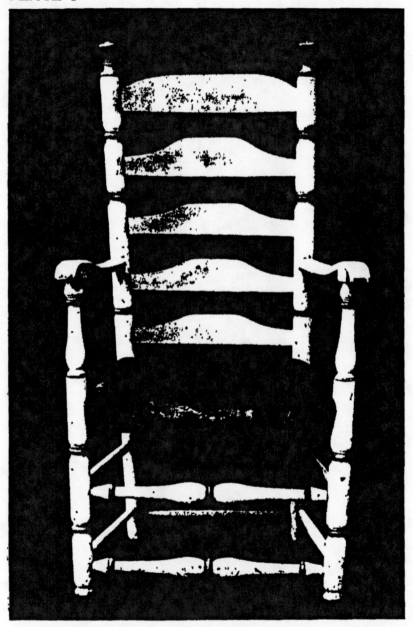

A LARGE AND FINE CHAIR OF ABOUT 1730, "AS FOUND"
Such a piece "in the rough" carries a convincing aura of age and authenticity

entire place again admiring the fine details of his choicest pieces, and, perhaps, reminiscently smiling as he recalls the troubles and difficulties of their capture. As the Captain of a Salvation Army post may honestly glow over the reclamation of some human wreck, so may the collector virtuously congratulate himself over the redemption of a fine old piece from a condition of wreckage and ruin to its present state of beauty, completeness, and utility. The big-game hunter, standing in his trophy-room and recalling each patient stalk and fortunate shot, has no advantage over the collector of American antiques.

To descend to more material considerations. A home completely furnished with good American antiques is no unimportant financial asset. If, for instance, a shrewd collector has, during the past decade, furnished such a house at a cost of, say, ten thousand dollars, using due care as to prices paid, he has a very sound asset, quickly and easily turned into cash. Probably such a collection would sell at auction for more than its original cost. On the other hand, ten thousand dollars invested in modern home furnishings is not a sound asset. If the owner found it necessary to dispose of such belongings, he would be fortunate indeed to realize a fifth of his investment. As an ancient and unique friend of mine in the country once observed: "Yes, sir, when you got a house full of good old stuff, you kin set right down front of the stove at night, light the pipe, and say—Well, I'm sure worth more tonight than I was this mornin'."

Chapter II

THE PHILOSOPHY OF RESTORATION

I SHALL assume that collectors of early American furniture intend their collections, either large or small, for actual use in their own homes. Furniture acquired for museum purposes might be considered from quite another angle. Household furniture will be put to strenuous daily service, while the furniture of a museum is for inspection only. A rash individual attempting to "try" a chair in the American Wing of the Metropolitan Museum will quickly discover that such specimens are not for use. What we want in our homes, therefore, is furniture that may really be used and may perfectly serve its purpose. It would, of course, please all of us to have affairs so arranged that we could acquire, at moderate cost, a collection of American furniture which needed no repairs of any kind. The individual pieces might need refinishing, but no repairs, new parts, or restorations would be required. Alas, such a happy condition is impossible unless to the few of us who need never consider price. The furniture we long to possess will be almost seventy-five to three hundred years old, and will, according to its age, have suffered a tremendous amount of use and abuse. An old English print pictures a cottage, at the front of which a man is loading his furniture into a wagon. Beneath appears the veracious legend, "Three removes are as bad as a fire." Much of the furniture which we unearth will have undergone more than three "removes." Many of our ancestors were restless, and much of their furniture endured considerable travel—particularly during the last century. By cart, wagon, pung, scow, sailboat, steamer, and railroad, it went hither and yon, and it is not surprising that much that has managed to survive now needs repair and restoration. It is

22

more surprising that we find so many pieces in fairly good condition.

Occasionally we meet an enthusiastic collector who proudly announces, "I never restore anything. I just bring the pieces home and stand them about, quite as I find them." I can understand such a point of view but as a policy for home-furnishing it seldom works very well. If we examine his collection, we discover it more or less wrecked, wobbly, and not in condition to do its duty. We find Windsor chairs whose backs come out with a touch, tripod stands propped in corners to hold them upright, drop-leaf tables with broken hinges, chests of drawers with their drawers stuck fast and brasses missing or broken. We find chairs so cut down that the seat may be no more than ten inches from the floor, trembling lowboys and highboys; beds, sofas, chairs in such a condition of decrepitude that they are liable, at any moment, to collapse under the startled visitor. Indeed, a lengthy stay in the midst of such furniture might be characterized as a dangerous adventure.

A POLICY NECESSARY

So our problem becomes: What do we want to collect and in what condition are we willing to accept our acquisitions? Shall we confine our attention to the later things which may often be found whole and sound; or shall we bring home the more or less wrecked earlier pieces which may require considerable restoration? Each collector must determine these matters for himself. However, we will find that the very early pieces are not easily found in any sort of decent condition, while the later pieces are much more easily acquired. The amount of restoration required will probably closely follow the ratio of age.

BE CAUTIOUS ABOUT WRECKS

Buying wrecks should be indulged in with caution, however, as many pieces are so mangled that only extreme rarity would warrant their purchases and restoration. And yet, if, on a fateful day, one of us discovers an American court cupboard in an ancient henhouse, he will hardly say to the farmer-owner, "No, my good man, I am not interested in your old cupboard. It is a quaint old cupboard, but it lacks various parts; and I want only entirely original pieces." A court cupboard might—to exaggerate—lack dozens and dozens of parts, and yet be most acceptable. Again, a Flemish armchair, a fine heart-and-crown or a Carver chair, or a six-leg highboy would—any one of them—warrant considerable restoration. We may say, then, *the greater the rarity, the greater the permissible restoration.*

There is, however, a certain class of furniture which warrants little or no repair. In this class we might place common three-slat-back chairs, Hitchcock chairs, late Windsor chairs of poor types, the common pine or tulipwood six-board chests, nailed cradles, washstands, the very common type of four-legged candlestands, the wooden-seat chairs of many styles, and all of the Victorian furniture of solid walnut.

Also of questionable desirability are many of the badly damaged mahogany-veneered pieces of early and late Empire style, bureaux, desks, sleigh beds, sewing-stands, and sideboards. These are all veneered pieces, and sometimes have been exposed to the weather, which has loosened the glue of the veneer; or possibly the veneer has broken off or been badly chipped in many places. In such cases restoration means much work and the finished result is usually patchy and unpleasing.

Veneered furniture suffers more from exposure and hard use than do similar types made of solid wood. A solid tulipwood chest of drawers might stand in a leaky shed for several years without serious harm, whereas a chest veneered with mahogany would be ruined by such exposure.

At auctions all sorts of common and badly wrecked pieces

sometimes sell at astounding prices to an enthusiastic and excited assemblage—such is the effect of mob psychology. With a little hunting among the shops, similar pieces may be found in good condition at very modest prices, and their rarity is not sufficient to warrant extensive restoration. These statements *do not*, of course, apply to the earlier and finer types of mahogany-veneered furniture, Hepplewhite and Sheraton sideboards or finely inlaid bureaux or card tables. Such pieces are not readily found and even if in poor condition are well worth considerable restoration. Neither of course does it apply to the rarest of collectibles, the walnut-veneered pieces of the late seventeenth and very early eighteenth century.

Time will probably continue to change our standards of rarity, as it has always done. Could we look forward to the year 1960, we might see a delighted collector showing to an envious brother his latest find—a real three-slat-back chair on which the only restorations are two new finials, three new slats, seven new rungs, and six inches added to the bottom of each leg. To hazard a guess as to the market price of pine washstands in that year is quite beyond my powers of prophecy.

We should very carefully examine in a good light every piece of furniture before purchasing, as hastily acquired pieces have an unfortunate way of showing, under careful scrutiny at home, about twice the amount of restoration that we had anticipated.

WHAT WE MAY FIND

If we have decided that thorough and honest restoration is permissible, let us consider some of the furniture that we may purchase subject to such restoration:

Tavern tables of many sorts: Tops, drawers, and feet may be missing; often some, or all, of the stretchers may have been sawed out.

Cabriole-leg Dutch-foot, and gateleg tables, in various stages of dilapidation.

The frames of butterfly tables, with or without the drawer.

Windsor chairs with a broken bow, or rail, with one or more spindles gone, or from two to four inches missing from the bottom of each leg.

Slat-back, fiddle-back and banister-back arm and side chairs, of many kinds, with finials, banisters, rungs, and often the entire set of lower rungs gone, and with rockers nailed on. (The craze for rockers certainly cost us many fine chairs, which might otherwise have come down to us intact.)

Desks, of many woods and designs, often with the feet missing, and, possibly, with lid and brasses gone.

High and low four-post beds, with two to eight inches cut from the bottom of each foot.

Highboys and lowboys, with drawers, feet, tops, or brasses missing.

Chests and chests of drawers, of innumerable kinds, with feet, tops, moldings, drawers, and brasses missing.

Looking-glasses, of all sorts. Those with wood frames will nearly all be veneered—the older styles with walnut, the later types with mahogany. Mirrors entirely gilded over a surface of plaster are common. These last are very difficult to repair when in bad condition, and will need professional attention. If a looking-glass has its original glass, and we intend it mostly for an ornament and not for use, the old glass, however cloudy and dull, should be preserved. This does not apply if we intend the looking-glass for actual service, as over a dressing-table.

All sorts of clocks—varying from the tall "grandfathers" to the late "steeple" clocks of the 1850's. Some of these will be of solid woods—maple, cherry, or walnut. The later types will probably be veneered with mahogany or rose-

PLATE 3

A MODERATE RESTORATION
Original except four lower rungs and about four inches added to each leg. Turned foot of rear legs probably incorrect

B MINOR RESTORATION
Small notches cut in feet to receive rockers have been filled. It is original single coat of green paint

C CONSIDERABLE RESTORATION

This trestle-foot, tuckaway, gateleg table, of maple, had no top when found, and the member which supports the bottom of the gate had, at some time, been crudely restored with black walnut. The feet are original. As restored, the top is a bit small. The table is of such rarity that its restoration is quite warranted

wood. They often occur merely as clock cases, minus face, hands, and works. Old clocks add greatly to a room, but, after some experience, I have little remaining faith in their accuracy, or their assistance in the prompt meeting of appointments.

In American mahogany, we shall find that the earlier pieces, like American Chippendale, Hepplewhite, and Sheraton chairs, ball-and-claw tables, lowboys, and high-boys, will be of solid, very heavy mahogany (commonly called "San Domingo"). Later we shall note mahogany veneer in use on bureaux, sideboards, tables, and articles displaying expansive flat surfaces. We shall, further, find many combinations in which the legs and frame are of solid mahogany, while the top, sides, and fronts are of mahogany veneer on pine.

Arriving at Empire times, we shall discover many pieces entirely veneered on all the visible surfaces, and we shall find combinations of solid maple frames, with sides, panels, or drawer fronts veneered with handsome curly, bird's-eye or burl maple, or these woods displayed in interesting and striking combinations with mahogany.

Nearly all American veneering will be found on a foundation of pine, although a few more costly pieces were occasionally made by applying the veneers to some fine wood— as a beautiful mahogany veneer on a foundation of mahogany, walnut or cherry. English cabinetmakers, in their work, were accustomed to use oak as a foundation for mahogany and walnut veneers, but the practice was by no means universal. Pine was frequently used. While, therefore, an oak carcase usually implies the English or Continental origin of a piece of furniture; the presence of pine is not accepted as proof of American making.

It is interesting to observe how, as time passes, veneer always tends to grow thinner. The walnut veneer of 1700 was sometimes one-tenth of an inch thick, while the mahogany veneer used in 1850 had been reduced, in extreme instances, to a thickness of one-fiftieth of an inch.

VICTORIAN FURNITURE

The term Victorian Furniture covers a wide variety of household pieces of mahogany, rosewood, and black walnut. We may find large bureaux with or without attached looking-glasses, parlor sets, matching sofa, arm and side chairs, tables with marble tops, their leaves and aprons elaborately carved, whatnots, desks, sleigh beds, ottomans, footstools, and huge sideboards. It was a period of mixed styles and influences. Traces of the ancient cabinetmakers—Empire, Gothic, Roman—"improved" with much carving, ornament, jig and fret-saw work, formed a mélange of style which seems to have delighted our grandparents. Almost all Victorian furniture was the work of furniture factories using machine methods and it was put together with glue and screws—wood pins were not employed.

The mahogany furniture is the most desirable of this period, but all Victorian objects have, for some time, interested certain collectors. If we wish to acquire this furniture, it may easily be found in very good condition and at modest prices.

Chapter III

SOME REMARKS ON RESTORATION

THE work of restoration may be done by oneself or by a cabinetmaker according to preferences and circumstances.

I myself have done all restoration on my own collection. The majority of my pieces are quite in original condition, and have required no repairs, while others were badly wrecked when acquired, and demanded much attention. I have thus had excellent and abundant opportunity to dissect old furniture, restore, and refinish it.

For extensive operations an elaborate equipment of tools is necessary, and some knowledge of their handling, or a natural aptitude for carpentry. If we are what is called "handy" with tools, we shall probably be successful with restoration; but if we cannot drive a nail straight, or saw on a straight line, we shall do better to leave our restoration to someone else. Even then a knowledge of the subject is of great value.

As with gardening, the playing of games, and other activities, restoration and refinishing calls for real effort. It requires much bending and working in strained positions. As a reducer of the waistline and as a general conditioner it is much superior to any "daily dozen" directed over the radio before breakfast. In gluing together an old armchair we need all of our hands, feet, and, maybe, as some wag has suggested, a trained octopus to hold the various arms, rungs, and parts in place during the process.

But the performance of these various operations develops *a really practical knowledge of the details of old furniture such as can be gained in no other way.* As in any other field, the knowledge gained by actual experience is always of

PLATE 4

A Heart and Crown Arm chair Both arms, four rungs, and about six inches of legs are restorations

B Maple Slat Arm chair Finials, four slats, lower rungs and six inches of legs restored

TWO EXAMPLES OF EXTREME RESTORATION

C CONNECTICUT RED OAK TAVERN TABLE OF ABOUT 1680–90
Feet, drawer, and one edge of top restored Rarity justifies considerable restoration

PLATE 4

A Heart and-Crown Arm chair Both arms, four rungs, and about six inches of legs are restorations

B Maple Slat Arm chair Finials, four slats, lower rungs and six inches of legs restored

TWO EXAMPLES OF EXTREME RESTORATION

C CONNECTICUT RED OAK TAVERN TABLE OF ABOUT 1680-90
Feet, drawer, and one edge of top restored Rarity justifies considerable restoration

Only occasionally, and then in rather late furniture, do we find evidence of slackness or poor workmanship. Mortise and tenon joints, hardwood pins, dovetails, and long hand-wrought nails combine in an ensemble well calculated for enduring usefulness through generations.

SPARING THE MARKS OF TIME

In the matter of restoration, we often have to consider pieces which have never been shortened with a saw, but have lost from one-half to two inches from wear. If an old piece is in fine condition except for this slight loss of height, it is, in my opinion, a mistake to restore the missing inch. By restoring in such cases, we remove the pieces from the class of *all original* to the class of *restored*; and the slight gain in appearance does not compensate for the change in classification. However, in deciding this matter we must, of course, be influenced by the character of the feet under consideration. A fine Spanish-foot chair which has lost one inch from its carved foot will have suffered a considerable diminution in grace and beauty, while a Windsor chair might bear the same depletion without any very noticeable harm.

Moreover, in all our restoration, let us not be too particular and finical about small details. In dealing with the older and cruder pieces especially let us do everything possible to save the smaller evidences of age and long usage—the old hand-wrought nails often driven into table tops when the pins came loose, burns, the marks of three-legged pots, old saw marks, crisscross knife marks, carved initials, and various and curious stains. All these things are *history* —a history whose writing may have required two hundred years or more to complete.

I have a secretary on whose slanting top some child once carved a rough ship and the name *Mary*. This secretary is more interesting to me with Mary's name on the lid than if the youthful indiscretion had been planed out.

A banister-back armchair has the initials *I.H.* and *A.B.* deeply carved in the left arm. It is a pleasing touch, and we may wonder who I.H. and A.B. were, where they lived, and when.

MAHOGANY REQUIRES SPECIAL TREATMENT

Mahogany furniture is, of course, of a finer and more formal character than many of the earlier and simpler pieces made of native woods. Mahogany furniture was never intended for use in the kitchen or for any rough wear. On the other hand, much of the earlier furniture of solid wood, which we now collect and prize so highly, was strongly built for daily use, often in workrooms. We cannot picture a housewife of 1765 seated in her kitchen preparing her evening meal before a mahogany table. Instead, she would doubtless have been employing a table of maple or pine, well worn, and scarred. If the home possessed any mahogany furniture it was *not* in the kitchen. Nor was the later mahogany of Hepplewhite, Sheraton and Phyfe intended for anything but formal purposes.

This being the case, it would seem that we should, in the restoration of mahogany, lean toward a more exquisite and more thorough restoration and refinishing than in the treatment of the furniture of solid native wood types. Nevertheless this does not mean that *every* sign of age should be removed even from our old mahogany. If I were the owner of the finest mahogany Chippendale armchair in existence, on the arm of which some old vandal had carved his initials, these initials would remain quite undisturbed.

Old table tops should be preserved, even if in rather bad condition. An original mahogany top, badly burned, stained, and marked, may not be entirely pleasing, but it is prefer-

PLATE 5

A CONSIDERABLE RESTORATION
About seven inches of right arm, one arm spindle, and
large hole in seat restored

Braced-back Windsor Chairs are rare and well worth restoration

B MODERATE RESTORATION
Original in every way except for about three inches added
to each bow

able to a new one. A maple tavern table with similar marks seems highly desirable.

Old table tops should *almost never* be planed, and we should not attempt to restore every tiny break, replace every lost splinter, or fill every tack hole. If, at times, we are forced to use a plane to remove deep burns or stains, let us prefer to use this tool lightly on our mahogany, cherry, walnut, and maple furniture.

A scraper may, at times, be a necessary instrument for cleaning old furniture. But what may be called "skinned furniture" is a common sight, these days—fine old pieces, whose entire outer surface has been quite removed by the scraper, supplemented perhaps, by the plane. Every nick, mar, or scratch has been removed until the piece has every appearance of a good reproduction. Such butchery is irreparable, and a piece so treated has lost a large share of its interest to a real lover of antique furniture.

We usually find that as a thoughtful and intelligent collector progresses along his chosen road, he feels an ever increasing aversion to the removal of the marks of age and use from his furniture. The newer collectors are very often inclined to demand that all antique furniture of every sort be scraped, skinned, and highly varnished. The moral of this paragraph is that if we wish even to simulate connoisseurship and experience we will not consider having six coats of shiny varnish applied to our court cupboards; nor submit our Flemish cane chair of maple to a bath of mahogany varnish stain. These things are simply not done in the best collecting circles.

BRASSES

In finishing pieces which carry the original brasses, *never* remove the brasses; all work should be done around them, leaving a bit of the old finish close to the edges, and retaining the marks of the brasses on the drawer fronts.

If the original brasses are removed and the drawer fronts thoroughly scraped, no one can afterward be at all certain that the brasses are really the original equipment: they might be old but not original. Cotter pin and drop handles were held in place by iron wires bent at a right angle and driven into the interior surfaces of the drawers. If the plates are removed for refinishing, these wires must all be pried out of the wood, and very often these marks of removal will cast a doubt over the originality of the mounts. A piece bearing a complete set of cotter pin or drop brasses is about as rare as the proverbial teeth of the hen. Even the later furniture with every one of its original brasses intact and in place is difficult to find. Original brasses, therefore, greatly enhance the value of any piece, and we should be very careful to do nothing to destroy the evidences of their originality.

A four-drawer piece which originally carried eight plates and handles and four keyhole escutcheons will perhaps lack two plates and as many handles. Under such circumstances we must send one of the old brasses to someone who will make, by hand, two exact replicas of the originals. Handmade brasses are inevitably expensive, but their cost is well warranted if it enables us to complete and use an original set. If, however, we find a piece which has none of its original hardware, let us not go hastily to our local hardware shop and buy a set of cheap, thin, shiny, and awful so-called "reproduction" brasses. Such additions will quite ruin the appearance of a really fine piece. Good reproduction brasses are easily obtainable at modest prices from dealers advertising in the magazines *Antiques* and *The Antiquarian*. Such brasses are correct in design, and are really reproductions of old patterns. They are also furnished in "old" or "antique" color, so harmonizing with our old furniture. We should make sure however, that any brasses purchased are of the proper style for the period of our furniture. A six-leg highboy of 1700 should not wear oval Sheraton brasses. A Shera-

PLATE 6

A   AN ENTIRELY ORIGINAL TAVERN TABLE
It has lost probably two inches from its height, but left in its present
condition it is "all original"

B   INITIALS AND MARKS ON THE ARM OF A MAPLE BANISTER-BACK CHAIR
It is well to preserve such interesting voices from the past

their arrangement will be found systematic and balanced. A tavern table with maple legs may have oak stretchers, pine skirt and top, and maple drawer front; but almost invariably, *all* of the legs will be of maple, *all* of the stretchers of oak, and the entire skirt of pine. If a Windsor chair has hickory spindles, they will, every one, be of hickory. All drawer fronts will be of the same wood. The backs of both the lower and upper parts of a chest-on-chest will be entirely of the same materials. If the left end board of a desk is of maple, the right end board will be of the same wood.

However, the usually logical arrangement occasionally becomes a bit disarranged. It seems that, at times, when our ancestors were constructing furniture which was intended to be *painted* at once, they become indifferent. If the proper wood was not at hand, they used a substitute, though never at the expense of strength. The excuse must have been that the paint immediately covered any discrepancies in the materials.

Hence, we are occasionally puzzled by a Windsor chair with three legs of maple and one leg of oak, a maple tavern table with two stretchers of maple and two of cherry, or a chest of drawers with three pine drawer fronts and one of butternut. These variations sometimes lead the collector to suspect that he is the victim of some hocus-pocus, but the piece which troubles him may be quite original in every way. Yet since furniture displaying an unbalanced mixture of woods is unpleasing when cleaned off and refinished, we may well pass it by as samples of the type unless the pieces are of great rarity. It is a happy fact that their occurrence is not common.

NO IMPROVEMENTS IN STYLE PERMISSIBLE

Of course *no* restoration work should attempt to improve or better the type of any piece of furniture. A tavern table lacking stretchers should not be supplied with turned

PLATE 7

A ORIGINAL COTTER PINS CLINCHED ON INSIDE OF A DRAWER OF ABOUT 1725
Brasses so secured should be left undisturbed

B UNBALANCED USE OF WOODS IN PEDESTAL OF TRIPOD TABLE
The pedestal and one leg are of Cherry, the two remaining legs are White Oak—unpleasing when cleaned and refinished

stretchers. A banister-back chair with missing crest should not be restored with a finely carved crest. When we have no ·means of knowing every detail of style of the original, we must lean toward extreme simplicity in our restoration. This requires strength of character. There is always the temptation to improve on the originals.

REFERENCE GUIDES TO STYLE

When we must decide on the details of style for restorations, *Furniture Treasury, Furniture of the Pilgrim Century,* and *American Windsors* by Wallace Nutting, *Colonial Furniture in America* by Luke Vincent Lockwood, and *American Furniture and Decoration* by Edward Stratton Holloway, will provide us helpful illustrations of genuine early American furniture. In a work such as this, it is quite impossible to consider all details of style; but, by a careful study of the illustrations in the five admirable books just named, we may gain a very clear idea of style, proportion, and detail.

From such works we may learn the correct size and thickness of table tops in relation to their bases, the shapes of table tops, the projection of the tops of six-board chests, and the various sorts of cleats and battens used at the ends of such tops—the graduated widths of slats in three-, four-, and five-slat-back chairs, varieties of turned and molded banisters for chairs, the proper type of chair arms; the shapes of the various styles of cabriole leg, the correct form of Dutch, Spanish, Flemish, claw-and-ball and French feet, the appropriate scrolling of the frames of highboys and lowboys, tables and chairs.

The details of all the turned parts of early furniture are accurately portrayed in hundreds of illustrations—finials, drops, posts, table legs, chair rungs, ball and turnip feet, as well as the fine turnings of Windsor chairs, legs, stretchers, and under-arm posts, and the intricacies of moldings and cornices, carving and reeding. No collector who has access to these books has any possible excuse to offer for bad mistakes of style or design in his work of restoration.* No tavern tables with claw-and-ball feet, no turnip-foot chests of drawers with glass knobs, no inlaid mahogany Sheraton chests with large ball feet will be allowed to add a high note of ghastly individuality to his collection. A sufficient production of such curiosities may be safely entrusted to our large manufacturers of modern furniture.

* Luke Vincent Lockwood's *Colonial Furniture in America* in 2 volumes priced at $30.00, is a carefully arranged, thoughtful, and scholarly history of the sequence of styles in the various articles of household furniture from the earliest times to the beginning of the nineteenth century. It contains over a thousand illustrations.

Wallace Nutting's *Furniture of the Pilgrim Century*, which contained pictures of articles of furniture and household equipment used in America prior to 1720, is now virtually superseded by the same author's *Furniture Treasury*, published at $25 the copy, which presents some 5000 illustrations of American furniture during the period 1620-1810, together with much descriptive matter. *American Windsors*, likewise by Mr. Nutting, is precisely what its name implies.

Edward Stratton Holloway's *American Furniture and Decoration: Colonial and Federal*, published at $5, containing 200 illustrations of specially selected fine furniture and giving particular attention to the development of styles.

These books are indispensable to the collector and the restorer of furniture.

Chapter IV

MATERIALS FOR RESTORATION

OLD WOODS FOR NEW PARTS

WHEREVER possible, restoration should be carried out with old wood and with the proper wood. Such a policy cannot be inflexible, however, as just the sort of old wood we need is not always available. Old wood is more necessary for certain restorations than for others. If we must replace a missing top or drawer front for a tavern table, we shall need boards with an old, stained, and used surface if our finished piece is to appear right. If a maple highboy needs a single new drawer front our completed piece will be more pleasing and harmonious if we can find a sound, old, worn maple board for the replacement. A drawer front of *new* maple in such a position naturally has a most annoying way of appearing new, and so in decided contrast to the other drawer fronts. Stain and treat it as much as we may, it remains new, and, to use an early American expression, it "sticks out like a sore thumb." If, however, our tavern table or our maple highboy requires new feet, we may use new maple for the purpose, if we have no old maple of suitable size. The new feet, having, of course, to be turned, or cut, from the solid wood, the finished feet will, in any case, everywhere show freshly worked surfaces, whether the wood is old or new. However, even in such an instance, I should prefer to use old maple for the feet, as it is of a darker shade than new wood and not so difficult to bring to the color of the older surfaces.

In cutting a molding, planing out a cleat or tavern table stretcher, in turning chair rungs, finials, drawer knobs, or feet of various sorts, old wood is best if it can be obtained. However, all these operations when carried out with *old*

39

wood leave entirely freshly worked surfaces so that the used and patinated surfaces are destroyed. The only advantage offered by the old wood lies in its darker color and thorough seasoning.

In restoring Windsor chairs we shall be forced to use some new material. Old hickory for spindles is very difficult to find and to work, and, unless we are fortunate enough to come across some suitable-sized old spindles, we shall be forced to shave our restorations out of new hickory. For a new comb, rail, or bow on a Windsor chair, where steaming and bending is required, we can only use new very straight grained ash, oak, or hickory, as *old wood* is so brittle that, after steaming, it will not stand the strain of bending.

When we consider the subject of mahogany furniture, I should always prefer the use of old wood, but a top of new mahogany on an old table, seems in a less painful state of disharmony with the older parts than does a top of new maple or pine on an old tavern table. Large surfaces of new maple or pine are only with great difficulty harmonized with original parts, and their use is seldom satisfactory.

So, as a policy in our restorations, let us decide, wherever possible, to use old materials—and, if we cannot find old materials, to use the best available new materials of the proper sort.

In almost any of our towns and cities are lumber dealers who can furnish us with any new woods we may want, even in small quantities. New tulipwood and western sugar pine boards in widths up to thirty inches are available. New clear native white pine is hard to find in wide boards, but the western sugar pine is a very good substitute. It is often difficult, in smaller communities, to find any mahogany of fine quality. The wood usually offered is *bay wood*, a very poor, coarse wood, light in color and weight, and not at all suitable for use on furniture.

PLATE 8

A COLLECTION OF OLD WOODS USEFUL IN RESTORATION

The J. H. Monteath Company of 204 Lewis Street, New York City, can furnish almost any sort of fine mahogany or other tropical woods, in solid form or in veneers.

I have had rare opportunities in my exploration of old barns, workshops, attics, and cellars, to obtain many kinds of old woods in all sorts of sizes, and at low prices. I have, for some time, made a practice of bringing home all sorts of odds and ends. In fact, on the last lap of some of these expeditions, my car has fairly bristled with old boards, beams, strips, bed rails, and table frames. At the time of acquisition much of this old material seems of little account, as it does not fill any immediate need. However, it is all carefully stowed away, and I now have such a large and varied stock of such material that I can usually find almost anything I need.

It is interesting to observe how this stock will often supply the exact width and thickness of board required. How two cuts from a worn old shelf will furnish a tavern table top of the proper width with worn and rounded edges, and with no use of plane or rip saw. How two one-inch strips, rip-sawed from the edge of an old board of suitable thickness, will furnish two fine worn cleats for the ends of this same top. An old three-quarter-inch pine board of exactly the right shade of brown may be found to replace part of the missing back of a mahogany chest of drawers—certainly a more pleasing restoration than if we had used a section of a new packing case bearing the printed warning, "Handle with Care—This Side Up." I have seen many drawers and backs of chests of drawers built of pieces of packing boxes adorned with interesting but inappropriately placed advertisements of mustard, pickles, soap, and other household necessities. Such material incorporated into the structure of any piece of antique furniture is certainly a blow to one's sensibilities.

OLD MAPLE

The best available source of old maple for small turnings is the odd end and side rails of old beds. These rails may often be purchased for trifling sums and they are most valuable in restoration work. The holes bored for ropes will interfere somewhat with our plans, but enough clear wood is left for almost any small turning. I have, in my collection of materials, several sections of fine straight-grained rock maple, eight feet long and five inches square. These are parts of an old carpet-loom and are clear and absolutely free from holes or mortices. At present I have no use for them, but, undoubtedly, a need will some day arise. I have several long bed rails four inches square of the very finest curly maple. As beautiful old curly maple is difficult to come by, these rails are being carefully treasured for a purpose at present unknown.

Old maple boards are also difficult to find and I recently saw a collector pay twenty dollars for a maple table, as he needed one of the drop leaves for the missing lid of a slant-top desk. However, we may, at rare intervals, find an old maple table top or six-board chest, and this material should be carefully treasured.

OLD PINE, TULIPWOOD, AND OAK

Dilapidated six-board chests will often furnish fine, wide pine and tulipwood * boards. Wrecked chests of drawers will give us materials for drawers and backs, and even old drawer runs may be saved and used. The kitchen tables of fifty years back, available in second-hand shops, will frequently furnish nicely worn pine and tulipwood tops.

* We use this name for the wood of the native tree Liriodendron Tulipifera, common throughout Connecticut, lower New York State, New Jersey, and Pennsylvania. This tulipwood is often called whitewood, as are also the similar woods of our native poplar and basswood Avoid any confusion with the West Indian Tulipwood, which is yellowy brown with longitudinal stripes of pinkish red and was considerably used for inlays and bandings in the times of Hepplewhite and Sheraton.

THE YIELD OF OLD HOUSES

Old and partially dismantled houses will often give us wide pine boards. I once so purchased some twenty-seven-inch pine boards which had been used as shelves in the "buttery." They were without a single nail hole or knot, beautifully brown, and had the old plane marks on the under side. They were the most delightful boards I have ever seen, and later served for the tops of tavern tables.

Old houses will also furnish us with plenty of oak from their hewn timbers and wide oak boards from their floors, although the floor boards are always marred by nail holes. They will occasionally supply old panels and moldings, for which a use may later appear. We may find in an old window-sash small panes of rough, greenish glass which will do nicely in the door of a china cupboard or as the side lights of the hood of a tall clock. A few handfuls of long hand-forged nails or the short nails which held in place the old-time riven laths will not come amiss. But it is an excellent plan, before obtaining any material from even the most dilapidated house, to secure the owner's permission for such procedure. Nothing is harder to explain in a nonchalant and convincing manner than one's presence with axe and crowbar in a house owned by a complete stranger.

CHAIR SLATS, BANISTERS, AND RUNGS

For replacing missing slats in slat-back chairs I have seen nothing that equals the rims of large wool spinning wheels. These rims are usually of ash or oak, and their curvature makes them work nicely into a chair slat, without any steaming or bending. The long bases of these wheels are very often made of the finest white oak, which may be of use to us.

Missing straight side banisters may be cut from old tulipwood or pine boards of the proper thickness.

Old ash is hard to find, but a used rake handle has been known to supply a rung in an early chair, and the large turned ash post of a great wool spinning wheel will answer for finials or feet for an ash slat-back chair, if we are so fortunate as to find such a chair.

Old oak and maple do not answer too well for the pins of mortice and tenon joints, as the old wood is sometimes rather brittle and small pins made of it have an evil way of breaking square off when we try to drive them into place.

OTHER OLD WOODS

Fine cherry boards, usually from the table tops of 1840 and 1850, seem very easy to discover in the second-hand shops. Yet, if we require a piece of old cherry two inches or three inches in diameter, we probably shall not find it.

We shall likely have little difficulty in securing old mahogany veneer which has become loosened from the surface of a ruined piece. Old veneer for small replacements is more satisfactory than new, as its color is dark. Mahogany boards from old table tops, both of the San Domingo and lighter mahoganies, may occasionally be found in second-hand shops.

Black walnut boards from Victorian furniture—the huge beds, bureaux, and tables—are easily procurable in second-hand shops.

The small jobbing carpenter-shops existing in all communities are likely to have on hand much miscellaneous old material, accumulated from their various operations. These stocks often contain old mahogany, walnut, maple, and pine, which may be purchased at less than the cost of new material.

And so my advice is to gather and save any good old woods and other materials for construction without regard to immediate necessity. If we wait until we need a certain

PLATE 9

A FINE ORIGINAL EXAMPLE OF THE BEST WINDSOR CONSTRUCTION
Maple, White Oak, Hickory, and Basswood—Unrestored

piece of old wood this will be the very thing we cannot locate, and we may use much gasoline and patience in the search for it. The time to acquire old woods is when fortune offers an opportunity, and not when we are actually in need of them.

Chapter V
SOME DETAILS OF RESTORATION

AS PREVIOUSLY remarked, each collector must decide just how deeply he wishes to go into the matter of personally equipping himself for and carrying out the restoration of his old furniture. We may, on the one hand, gather together a simple outfit for lesser repairs, nailing loose moldings, restoring lost chair rungs, or gluing loose parts in place; or, we may set up an electric turning lathe, power saw, and a complete equipment of all the necessary tools for all possible operations. Not many collectors will likely go to the latter extreme, as few of us have the necessary time, inclination, or natural aptitude for handling tools required by such a course.

However, we may be very sure that if we can arrange matters so as to do a considerable amount of our own work, we shall, in this way, gain such knowledge of all the structural details of antique furniture as can be gained in no other way. We shall learn to know at a glance the difference between the methods of construction of the years 1710 and 1810. All of those structural features which often remain a dark mystery to many collectors will become clear to us. Our growing knowledge, further, will not be based on theory, hearsay, or legend. With such knowledge at our command, many of the sweeping verbal and printed statements about American furniture which we encounter will seem rather ridiculous, and we shall be always ready for a friendly tilt with a brother collector, because we shall know whereof we speak.

Naturally it is impossible within our allotted space to treat the thousand details of all the furniture styles of the long period between the years 1620 and 1850, nor is it necessary.

PLATE 10

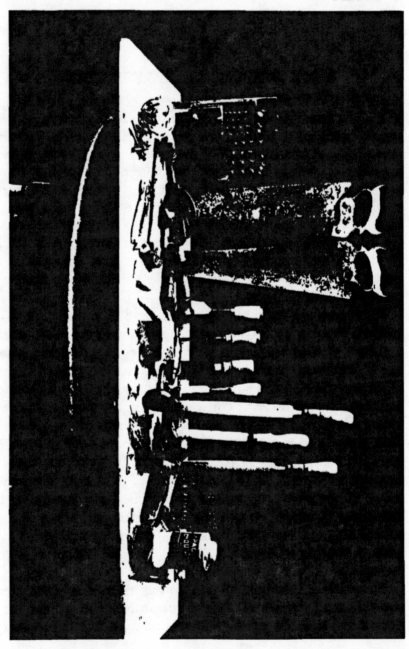

AN OUTFIT OF TOOLS SUFFICIENT FOR THE EXECUTION OF CONSIDERABLE RESTORATION

Many pieces requiring our care will be sufficiently intact themselves to answer any questions as to their style. If a Windsor chair has lost a single leg, we still have the remaining three as patterns, and need no illustration as to the proper turning. But a "Chippendale" looking-glass minus its tall crest gives us no answer as to what this crest should be. When pieces have entirely lost stylistic details, we may well follow the previous suggestions as to consulting the authorities on style and period. As an alternative we should examine the collections of our friends and of the museums. We should not guess as to stylistic details, nor allow others to do this guessing for us, as they often seem very willing to do.

There are certain basic means and methods which apply to all restoration work.

GLUES AND GLUING

With the exception of its employment on veneering, we find little evidence of any considerable use of glue or other adhesive on our very early furniture. Not until after the Revolution shall we note any great dependence upon it as a means of holding together mortice and tenon or dovetail joints.

Le Page's Liquid Glue is fairly satisfactory for restoration work. It needs no heating and is always available. However, for large and important operations, the best stick glue, dissolved in water and applied hot, is stronger and more durable. This entails a glue-pot and means of heating and, so, is rather a nuisance.

Any attempted gluing operation without accompanying pressure is usually unsuccessful. Neither can we hope properly to glue varnished, painted, or oily surfaces, or the end-grains of wood. Whenever we use glue we should exercise great care immediately to wipe off any surplus with a damp cloth. Glue, when dry, remains practically untouched by varnish remover and if we leave a piece smeared and daubed

with the adhesive we shall, in our later cleaning-off operations, have much trouble in getting rid of this unnecessary
and flintlike substance.

Successfully to glue two surfaces together we must have
a fairly perfect contact of clean, dry wood, and the two parts
should be held in place with clamps until dry.

WORKING OR ROCKING GLUE INTO JOINTS

We may often find pieces of furniture whose shaky and
rickety condition plainly indicates that they need glue, and
yet they cannot be taken apart without considerable marring
and damage and the destruction of the old pins. Sometimes
slat-back chairs, pinned through every rung and slat, will
be quite intact and yet very shaky.

The back of a rickety fan-back Windsor may be fastened
both at the top and bottom by iron brads or wooden pins
run through the ends of each spindle. On an early tavern
table in which the stretchers are of the same square as the
posts, we cannot get at the rear ends of the pins which hold
the stretchers, if we wish to drive them out. Sometimes chair
rungs were turned with a slight bulb where the rung was
inserted into a green or unseasoned leg. Such a joint, under
the strains of use, will sometimes develop into a sort of
toggle joint—it will move about freely but cannot be taken
apart without splitting the posts.

All such shaky furniture may be treated by applying glue
about all the joints, working in all the glue we can with
a very thin splinter of tough wood or a narrow strip of thin
steel, and then rocking the piece back and forth in different
directions. It is surprising how persistence in this motion
will cause the glue to penetrate all the loose joints. If a table
is to be treated thus, the top should first be removed so as
to allow more "play" in the various joints.

This method of strengthening is not recommended as a
substitute for the usual process of driving out the pins and

taking the piece apart; but it may be used in special cases. It offers one great advantage—the old pins remain intact, unmarred, and undisturbed.

All the parts of any piece glued by this unprofessional method should be carefully fastened into correct position or the piece may dry into a strange and contorted shape. Ordinarily, long clamps are employed for this work; but a rope tourniquet may often be used on chairs and tables, as shown in our Plate 11, A. By this method we simply tie a soft strong rope about the piece in several places, leaving slack enough for an old chair rung or stick to be inserted and the rope tightened by twisting, precisely in the manner taught to the Boy Scouts for the treatment of wounded limbs. A strong, even pressure may be obtained with such a tourniquet and it may be used in various restoration processes. For pulling together all the joints in the underbody of a Windsor chair, with a single operation, it is perfection. An old marble table top is easily acquired and is very valuable to give us an exactly flat surface on which to place chairs or small tables which have been reglued.

DRILL BEFORE USING NAILS OR SCREWS

If anywhere we need to use screws, hand-wrought nails, or wire brads, holes slightly smaller than the diameter of these implements should be drilled in the wood. This drilling may not be essential on soft woods, such as pine, but is most important on old and hard woods, like maple, mahogany, and walnut. The attempted insertion of screws, nails, or brads into these woods without first drilling a suitable hole will very often result in splitting.

Screws, of course, should never be used where their heads will be visible when the piece of furniture is finished and in use. If the use of wire brads is indicated on any visible surface, their heads should be sunk with a nail-set and the openings filled with plastic wood or stick shellac.

In many restorations and repairs in locations subject to great strain very small screws will hold much better than wire brads. Size two and size three wood screws in lengths of five-eighths, three-quarters and seven-eighths of an inch are very useful. If a cracked arm rail of a Windsor chair is first glued and clamped, and later strengthened with two or three of these tiny screws, the repair is very likely to be permanent. Many other uses for these screws will suggest themselves.

Various sizes of straight mending plates and angle plates of steel, bored and countersunk for screws, may be used in hidden positions on old furniture for additional stiffening and strengthening, but they should not be employed as a substitute for the right sort of restoration work.

VARIOUS ORIGINAL FEATURES

It was customary, on nearly all old turned chairs, to score lightly with a chisel the exact points on chair posts and legs where, later, the holes were bored for the insertion of rungs, and where mortices were cut to receive the tenons or slats of the back members. These marks may be faint or deep, but they are nearly always present. If a Windsor chair requires a new leg, and the original legs are thus scored, the new turning should, for the sake of uniformity, be similarly marked.

The pins used on our early furniture were of course always made from hard strong woods such as oak, maple, beech, cherry, and walnut. These pins ranged in size from the tiny sorts of not more than one-sixteenth of an inch in diameter, used in Windsor and other chairs, to the massive half-inch pins of some of the heavy tables. That section of the pin intended to be first inserted was roughly rounded, gradually becoming approximately square or irregularly rectangular toward the outer end or head. *Perfectly round or turned pins were seldom used.*

PLATE 11

A ROPE TOURNIQUET HOLDING GLUED MEMBERS IN PLACE

B A SHERATON CHAIR WHICH HAS LOST ABOUT FOUR INCHES IN HEIGHT AND SHOULD BE RESTORED

When the roughly shaped pin was driven home, the corners of the upper section bit into the edges of the pin hole and made a tight, firm joint. On Pennsylvania furniture we may often see large, sharply oval pins of a sort seldom used in New England construction. Pins on old furniture will often be found projecting a bit beyond the wood which surrounds them. On reproductions, restored pieces, and frauds, the pins are nearly always cut off flush and are frequently exactly round. If we are forced, in our restoration work, to use any new pins, we should follow the old methods of making them, and not have their ends appear as a perfect circular spot on the finished surface.

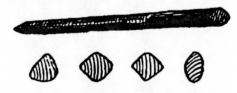

Fig. 1.   Old Wooden Pins

Old pins in unrestored furniture were seldom glued in place and they may be driven out with a wire spike of suitable size with its end filed square. The round pins of reproductions, rebuilt pieces, and frauds, are usually glued firmly in place, as are all mortice and tenon joints. *If, in restoration work, it is necessary to remove old pins, each pin should be laid systematically aside, so that it can be returned not only to the proper hole, but to its original position in the hole.*

There is a theory, mentioned by Lyon,* that the tenons were held in the mortices of very early furniture by a method called the "draw bore pin." Using this method, the hole through the tenon would be bored slightly nearer to the shoulder than was the hole through both sides of the mortice. Thus, when the pin was driven, it pulled the three

* "Colonial Furniture of New England."

bored sections into coincidence and formed an extremely tight joint. Such a method would naturally give each pin a kink. This "draw bore pin" may have been sometimes used, but I am certain that it was not *always* used, as I removed many old wooden pins which were perfectly straight and without any kink whatsoever. When old pins are removed from a mortice and tenon joint they will often be bent, sometimes so badly bent that their removal is difficult. I have noticed, however, that if a piece is very loose and rickety, the pins will have much more bend in them. This bend would be the natural result of wrenching strains on the pins, and it is possible that the kink of the supposed "draw bore pin" is the result of strain and not the result of any intentional difference in the boring of holes through the mortice and the tenon.

Genuine old furniture shows a complete lack of sharp knifelike edges on all parts which, through their location, were subject to much wear. The finials, feet, slats, banisters, rungs, and arms of chairs, the edges and corners of table tops, the edges of stretchers and the posts of tables, old moldings, and the feet of all sorts of furniture will be rounded and worn. This fact should always influence any restoration work that we may undertake, and nowhere on such work should we allow sharp edges or points to remain when the work is completed.

The matter of the warping of certain parts of old furniture, such as table tops, may give us some trouble. There are various means and complicated methods for attempting to take out this warp, but I must confess that they do not often give permanent results. It is an easy enough matter to straighten a warped board by dampening the concave side with water and exposing the convex side to the direct rays of the sun or the heat of a stove, but if it is so located that it cannot be held flat, it will very soon re-develop its old curve. If the drop leaf of a table has a decided warp,

we may easily correct it, but, unless some cleats are applied
on the under side, the correction will not be durable. A
warped table top is not at all distasteful to me. I own a
maple "beehive" table whose thick top undulates in a series
of most interesting curves and waves, and these will be allowed to remain undisturbed as an example of what maple
can accomplish if left to its own devices.

Three sorts of small moldings were often used for ornament about the drawers and in various positions on our early
furniture of native woods.

The single arch mold (A) is considered the oldest type.
The double arch mold (B) and the canal
mold (C) are believed to be a bit later. Moldings were usually held in place with very
small iron brads, but occasionally with tiny
wooden pins. These moldings were not strong,
and sections are often missing from our furniture. If we need any for our work, almost any
woodworking shop can produce the quantity
desired.

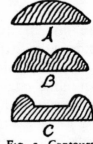

Fig. 2. Contours
of Moldings

USING THE SAW

Any joints which are required should of course be smooth
and even and properly sawn. When a board is cut off with
a saw, the lower edges of the cut are more ragged than the
upper edges, so we should arrange that the side of the
board which we intend to show on the surface of our finished piece shall be placed uppermost when sawn.

FILLING HOLES AND CRACKS

Sometimes we find large knot holes or decayed spots
which seem too large to fill with plastic wood. A suitable
sized rectangular block of wood with its grain uniform in
pattern and direction with the surrounding wood should be

set into such a surface and glued. This block may later be planed off flush.

We shall probably find some bad nail or small knot holes, cracks, or other places which will require filling. This may be accomplished with stick shellac, which is a composition much like sealing wax, to be had in such a variety of colors that the shade of any sort of wood, light or dark, may be closely matched. This shellac is melted in by pressing with a suitably hot iron or knife blade. It is much used on the better maple and mahogany furniture where the owner desires every hole smoothly filled because the piece seems to demand a rather fine finish.

A material for filling, called "plastic wood," is on sale at most paint stores. It is, I think, a combination of finely ground wood-pulp and some quick-drying agent like lacquer. Plastic wood dries very quickly and may be planed, sandpapered, and carved like wood. When dry, it is very hard and strong, and may be stained. Plastic wood may be tinted before using, by working in a little decorator's color (see Chapter VII) of any desired shade. When we become familiar with the properties of plastic wood on restoration work, innumerable uses for this material will suggest themselves. I consider it a very valuable filling, superior in every way to putty or a mixture of fine sawdust and glue, both of which are sometimes used for this purpose.

Usually all filling is done *before* cleaning off or smoothing. However, if we intend to use lye or savogran mixed with water for this cleaning we shall be wise to do the necessary filling *after cleaning-off*, as the water is likely to disturb or wash out any substance used for filling.

Otherwise all restoration should be quite finished and complete before any attempt is made to clean off the old piece. If this procedure is followed, the new parts will become so stained with the old finish, or paint, as this is removed, as more or less to harmonize with the old color of the piece. This makes it easier to match old and new surfaces in the final finishing.

RESTORING TABLE TOPS AND LEAVES

One of our most common necessary restorations is the replacement of tops on various styles of drop-leaf tables. Sometimes the entire top may be missing. In other cases, one or both drop leaves have disappeared. If we except certain tables which come in pairs or threes, and which sometimes have an unbalanced arrangement, such as a round drop leaf on one side and a square one on the other side, the tops of virtually all old drop-leaf tables may, roughly, be placed in four classes as to shape—round, short ellipse, long ellipse, and square or rectangular, the corners of the two latter styles being sometimes cut into ornamental shapes or merely slightly rounded.

The central section of a drop-leaf table may be wide or narrow in proportion to the width of the leaves, and the corners of the square variety may be rounded a bit, or cut into ornamental designs; but nearly all our drop-leaf tables will come within these four classes.

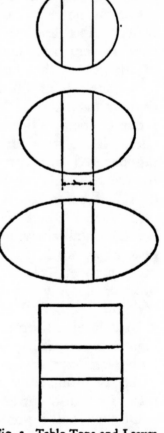

Fig. 3. Table Tops and Leaves

It will readily be seen in the illustrations of the round and elliptical types that the two ends of the central top sections are *always* cut on a curve and are *never* straight. If, on any tables within these three classes, the drop leaves are missing, we may quite accurately calculate the shape of these leaves by the curve of the ends of the central section which remains.

On a drop-leaf table of the square or rectangular sort, the central section has, of course, a straight edge, and any addition of half-round or half-elliptical leaves to a square central section is almost certainly incorrect. Considerable confusion seems to have arisen as to the correct shapes for the restored tops of drop-leaf tables, and many faulty and inaccurate examples of such restoration are encountered. Of course, where

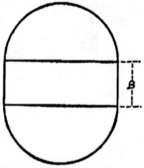

the entire top is missing, we can only consult the authorities on style as to the probable shape and size of the original top. We may obtain some evidence as to the probable width of the drop leaves if the parts which supported these leaves are still in place. These supporting members would, of course, be shorter on a round table than on one with a long elliptical top.

Fig. 4. Incorrect Restoration of Table Top

On many drop-leaf tables the support was furnished by a gate, or by movable legs which were hinged to the frame, but even when these supports were fully extended, they were still several inches from the edge of the leaf.

There are only three kinds of joint to consider in drop-leaf tables.

The square joint (1) is a plain square joint and the two boards butt squarely together. Some authorities say that this joint was never used on very early tables, and may be found only on unimportant tables of the mid-nineteenth century or on restorations. However, I have seen it on some simple early tables whose tops appeared to me to be quite original.

The tongue-and-groove joint (2) is the joint found on many very early gate-leg and butterfly tables. When the leaf is down, this joint leaves a very evident opening, yet its presence delights the collector, and it is counted earlier than the rule joint (3). It is probable that little use of the tongue-and-groove joint was made after the year 1725, as at that time the rule joint was in sway and its advantages in appearance caused a rapid displacement of the earlier style.

The rule joint (3), which, by its construction leaves no opening when the leaves are lowered, has, from early times,

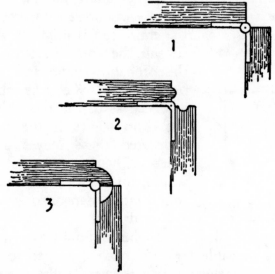

Fig. 5.   Drop-leaf Table Joints

been the joint most employed on American drop-leaf tables. This joint has been in continuous use since early in the eighteenth century, and is found on almost all modern tables.

We may find two, three, or four hinges at each joint of drop-leaf tables. The very early hinges were often of the forged *butterfly* type, fastened with short hand-wrought iron nails, sometimes clinched or riveted on the upper surface of the leaves. Later, hand-forged square hinges were used, fastened with square-end screws. When we encounter drop-leaf tables with heavy square *cast*-iron hinges, we may safely assign them to the nineteenth century.

When we must decide as to the thickness of old table tops, we can only be guided by illustrations and by the fact that the smaller the table the thinner the wood of the top is likely to be. The top of a small table might be five-eighths of an inch thick, while that of a large one a flush one-inch thick. Often, on small tavern tables and pedestal candlestands, with round or elliptical tops, rather heavy wood was

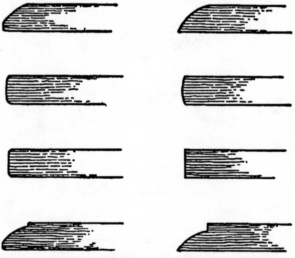

Fig. 6. Correct and Incorrect Edges of Table Tops

employed and the under edge was chamfered off, thus giving a lighter appearance while gaining the strength of thickness.

I have often seen small tables restored with square-edge tops one and one-quarter inches thick, and the effect is decidedly clumsy and unpleasant. As to the overhang on tables, we should consult the authorities on style as a wide variation existed in this matter. We may say, however, that tables with small frames seldom had huge tops, and tables with large frames usually carried tops with considerable overhang.

The edges of all sorts of table tops are often improperly restored so as to appear with sharp, knife edges, such as no old used table top could possess. The molded, the oval, the square, and the thumbnail molds are the four edges we shall commonly meet, and our illustrations show the right and wrong appearance of each. The thumbnail molding which was much used, not only on table tops but in many other locations, is particularly unpleasant when left with sharp edges and a deep shoulder, as in the second illustration.

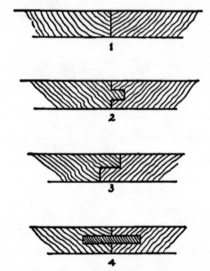

Fig. 7.   The Joining of Boards of Table Tops

JOINING THE BOARDS OF TABLE TOPS

When tables were of a dimension requiring a two-board top, a variety of methods were employed to fasten these boards together.

1. The *square butt* joint, sometimes glued on later types.

2. The common *tongue and groove* joint—an old device, but still used for almost all modern matched lumber.

3. The *ship lap* joint was sometimes used on tables, but

its use was not common. It will more likely be found on the backs of cupboards and chests.

4. The *double groove and tongue* joint was formed by cutting two deep grooves into the edges of the boards, into which a separate tongue was fastened by means of pins or glue. Its occurrence is not common on very early tables, but it was frequently employed on fine pieces after the year 1750.

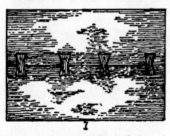

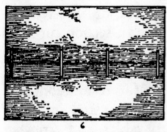

Fig. 7A. The Joining of Boards of Table Tops

5. The *mortise and tenon* joint was formed by cutting double and corresponding mortices, into which a sufficiently long tenon was inserted and held by wooden pins. This produces a fine, strong, unwarping joint and may be found on very early pieces. It was also used on later productions, usually of the better sorts.

6. The *doweled* joint was made by boring corresponding holes into which round pins were fastened. This joint will be found on many tops of widely divergent ages. It is commonly used on modern furniture.

7. The *double butterfly* joint was made by "letting in" small double wedge-shaped sections of wood into the under surface of the edges of the two boards to be joined. These wedges were sometimes glued, but were usually held in place by small wooden pins or brads. This butterfly joint we often find in various other locations where a sufficient width could not be secured in a single board—the ends and

tops of large chests, the ends of highboy tops, and in the wide leaves of large drop-leaf tables.

This class of tables covers a delightful variety of sizes and styles, ranging from the extremely rare and valuable oak tables of the seventeenth century to the smaller and more easily found sorts so much in use throughout the eighteenth century. Tavern tables were turned out in large numbers and were the favorite tables in the kitchens of the old homes, where they suffered much rough treatment. They often come to us minus tops, drawers, and feet.

The loss of height, through wear, decay, or the use of the saw, may, in extreme cases, be so great that the stretchers rest squarely on the floor. One, two, three, or all stretchers may have been removed with the saw, or a section cut from the rear of the top, so that the edge at that point is flush with the frame.

Tavern tables are common subjects for restoration, and such work is often accomplished in careless and improper ways. The tops of the small tavern tables and stretcher stands were square, round, oval, octagonal, or rectangular, and were often formed of a single board. These small oval and round tops had considerable overhang and were usually stiffened with a central cleat set across the grain of the top to prevent the edges from breaking off. The larger tavern tables were more likely to have rectangular tops made of two boards with some sort of cleat at each end of the top to prevent warping and splitting. Our illustrations show the four common methods of applying these end cleats:

1. The very common method of fastening by means of wooden pins, driven into holes drilled through the cleat and three or four inches into the ends of the top boards.

2. Also a common method: that of inserting long hand-

forged nails through the cleat and into the ends of top board. This was a better method than the first, as the iron nails were much stronger than wooden pins and broke less easily. It is interesting to observe on such a top, how the cleats will be very deeply worn *between* the immediate areas protected by these nails. Such a cleat may present the appearance of a series of shallow' waves with the nail heads at their crests.

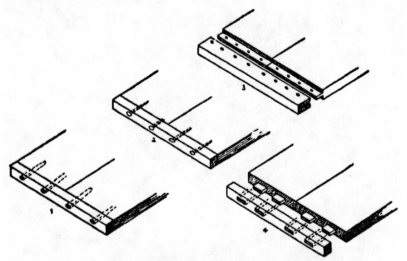

Fig. 8.   End Cleats on Old Tavern Table Tops

3. A less common method: that of cutting across the end of the top a wide tongue which was inserted into a corresponding groove in the cleat and fastened with wooden pins.

4. A rather uncommon method: that of cutting a number of tenons on the end of the table top and matching mortices in the cleat, fastening with wooden pins through the tenons.

The last two constructions produce strong, unwarping tops. Both are likely to be found only on the finer examples, more particularly on the tables of Pennsylvania, and *seldom on New England pieces.*

PLATE 12

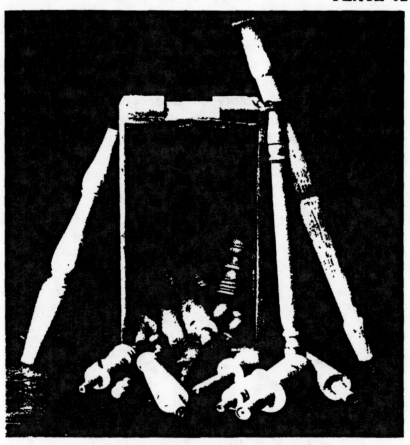

A. AN ASSORTMENT OF NEW TURNINGS FOR RESTORATION USE

B. TURNINGS FOR RESTORING CHAIR-LEFT

The restoration of missing feet on tavern tables is often necessary.

It was not the inflexible rule, but the rather customary practice on tavern tables, to place the stretcher in the centre of the lower squared section of the posts, leaving the stretcher equidistant between the shoulders of the turnings, A—B. The turnings are not always, but very often, the same in design below the stretcher as above, as shown in our drawing.

The feet may have only suffered a slight loss, as through line C; a more severe loss, as through line D; or a total loss, leaving the stretchers resting flat on the floor, as through line C. With such a complete loss, we of course have no means of being sure as to the exact pattern of the missing feet. However, as the pattern of the turning below the stretcher was very often exactly the same as that above the stretcher, except for the addition of a round or oval extremity, we are perfectly safe in thus arranging the restoration.

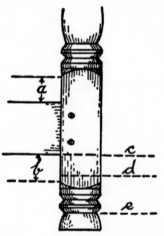

Fig. 9. Foot and Stretcher of Tavern Table

We should bear these matters in mind, and we may properly restore any degree of loss in these feet. We commonly meet with restored tavern tables improperly adorned with various sorts of strange feet, as in drawing A, having a long turned foot of a design quite out of accord with the design of turning above the stretchers.

It will almost invariably be found that, if the post of a tavern table be turned above the stretcher, it is also turned below the stretcher. Therefore, any tavern table restored with a square foot below the stretcher, as in drawing B will be pretty certain to have been wrongly treated. The square-leg tables, quite without any turning, should never be restored with turned feet. The feet should be square sections of wood to accord with the posts.

I have seen a number of tavern tables restored with a ball or bulbous foot, as in drawing C, which is, of course, quite incorrect.

We may carefully estimate the length and design of the new sections for the feet of tavern tables and have them turned with a pin of five-eighths-inch diameter and two inches long on the upper end. The lower end of the old legs should

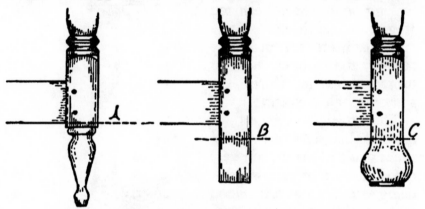

Fig. 10.   Incorrect Restorations of Tavern Table Feet

then be sawed squarely off, a hole of the right size bored in their centres, and the turned pins on the new feet inserted and glued firmly in place. It is best to so estimate that the new feet will be a little larger than necessary to cover variations in size and inequalities of shrinkage in the old legs. Any discrepancies between the old and new sections may be equalized after the feet are in place and the glue is dry.

Tavern tables which have lost their stretchers are often improperly restored with narrow stretchers as in Fig. 11. At point A, the outer face of the stretcher should be set even with the *outer face* of the square section of the post. When the upper frame members of a tavern table are set flush with the faces of the posts; the stretchers are also similarly placed.

RESTORING CHAIRS

Very often one or more banisters will be missing from old banister-back chairs. The split turned variety, which exactly coincides in pattern with the turnings of the back posts, may be of ash, oak, maple, or some other hard strong wood. I have never seen split turned banisters of tulipwood or pine. Soft wood in so small a turning would have been too fragile for such use. These split banisters are made by sawing the proper sort of turned section lengthwise, exactly through the centre.

The *straight* types of molded banisters are sometimes made of maple, but very often of pine or tulipwood— being straight, a soft wood was considered of adequate strength. As there was a wide variety of reeding and molding planes, we find many patterns of reeding and molding

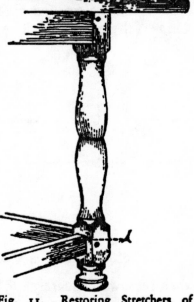

Fig. 11. Restoring Stretchers of Tavern Tables. The Stretcher Is Incorrect

on these straight banisters. If we need molded banisters and have not on hand one of the complicated planes now made for such purposes, we may call on a professional to turn them out to our patterns.

Missing slats from two-, three-, four-, and five-slat chairs may be very nicely restored with sections of the wide rims of the large wool spinning wheels. These wheels may often be purchased for trifling sums, and the rims are usually of oak and ash of about the required thickness for chair slats. The curvature of these rims allows us to fashion a slat without any steaming or bending. If we should require a maple slat, it may be steamed and bent, as we describe in the restoration of Windsor chairs, or we may readily find a slat from a dismantled slat-back chair.

The methods described for restoring missing feet on tavern tables are applicable to restoring lacking feet of turned chairs. The bottoms of the rear legs of old turned chairs are, nearly always, *a plain turned cylindrical section*, while the front feet should conform to the pattern of the turnings in the upper sections of the front posts. A comparison of the chair we wish to restore with illustrations in the works of Nutting, Lockwood, and Holloway should quickly show us the proper design for any lost feet. Yet, as is the case with tavern tables, we shall note many turned chairs improperly restored with curious and inappropriate feet. The new feet of chairs should be turned with a pin of five-eighths-inch diameter at the top, and should be glued into a hole bored into the bottom of the old posts.

The loss of the finials from turned chairs is a most serious one. Unless a chair is of impressive size or great rarity we should hesitate about buying a specimen thus mutilated. However, if chair finials must be restored we should consult the authorities on style, and choose the design for our finial which seems the right one. Finials should be turned with a pin, and applied in the same manner as the feet of turned chairs.

Dutch Feet and Spanish Feet are, of course, not turned, but are worked out of the solid wood. In restoring these a piece of wood of suitable size and partly shaped is set with a pin into the end of the old leg, and, when the glue is dry, the foot is worked down to exact size and shape with coarse wood rasps and other suitable tools.

It may be remarked that any amateur furniture restorer

PLATE 13

A. SINGLE BROAD DOVETAIL FROM TAVERN TABLE DRAWER OF ABOUT 1700
Nailed in place with hand-forged nails

B. EARLY DRAWER FRONT, RABBETED AND NAILED FROM THE FRONT WITH
HAND-FORGED NAILS

who sets out to restore a Dutch-foot table or highboy which has lost all of its feet and six inches of each leg, will be aware, before the work is finished, that he has attempted "some job."

Any sort of foot which is not turned may be restored by gluing on a suitable block and afterward cutting and working it down to the required size and shape. Square-tapered, round-tapered, spade, Dutch, ball-and-claw, scroll, and Spanish feet are all treated by this method, but to finish off the last three varieties some knowledge of carving is needed.

A very common restoration is replacing the missing feet on tripod-foot tables and stands. On such pieces, instead of doweling on a block, it is best to "halve on with glue" a suitable sized piece of wood, arranging matters so that the longitudinal joint comes at the side of the repaired leg. After the glue is dry, the lower part of leg and foot may be worked down to the proper shape and two or three tiny screws set into the lower side of the joint. These little screws at such a point are most valuable aids in preventing a later loosening of the glued joint.

DRAWERS

Often we may find pieces which have lost one or more drawers. Very early examples will probably have flush drawers, the lipped drawers being a later type, followed again later by flush drawers.

SIDE-RUN USED PRIOR TO 1700

The very early drawers were made with a groove at the side, this engaging a strip of wood fastened to the frame. It is most unlikely that we shall come across many pieces of American furniture of so great an age as to be constructed with side-run drawers.

Almost all drawers likely to come into our hands will slide on bottom runs fastened to the frame at each end. On some pieces we may find the drawer arranged to slide on a wide slat or board, placed in the centre of the drawer; but such construction is unusual. The sides of the very earliest drawers were rabbeted and nailed, or very broad dovetailing nailed in place appears. Many variations occur: drawer sides rabbeted and nailed to the front; only nailed at the back; broad dovetailing nailed at the front; and rabbeted and nailed at the back.

Dovetailing in cabinet work grows progressively narrower and finer as time passes until about 1800, the sides of nearly all drawers were fastened at all four corners with small dovetailing glued in place. Narrow and small dovetailing may be safely considered an evidence of relatively late work.

The bottoms of *very early* drawers were nailed to the sides. *Later*, the bottoms were nailed through the sides of the drawers, the front edge being thinned off and inserted into a groove cut in the drawer front. *Still later*, the bottoms were thinned down on three edges which were inserted into grooves cut into the front and sides, while the fourth edge was nailed to the back.

The last method of construction was commonly used in the mahogany furniture of the Hepplewhite, Sheraton, and Empire periods. The early flush drawers stood use and wear much better than the lipped drawers, which often have badly broken edges and corners. Frequently the lip at the end of the drawer has, in breaking off, carried away several inches of the front surface of the drawer. Such a piece is a pest, and, unless it is of some rarity, we may do well to pass it by. If we try to go over a chest of four badly damaged lipped drawers and restore all their edges, we shall find it tiresome work with a patchy and unpleasing final result. However, if such work is necessary, we may set in narrow strips of wood to replace the lost lips, later bringing

PLATE 14

A FAIRLY WIDE DOVETAILING ON DRAWER OF BALL-FOOT CHEST
OF ABOUT 1725
Corner pin Brasses

B NARROW DOVETAILING TYPICAL OF LATENESS
From a Mahogany Bureau of about 1840

them down to proper size with a rabbeting plane and sandpaper.

We shall frequently find pieces in which broken lips have been planed off so that the drawer front is flush. Sometimes the edges will have been molded in simulation of a lip; sometimes treated to look as if they had a beaded edge. Such pieces are not desirable.

The drawer runs on old pieces are often badly worn and the drawers do not slide properly. Although we dislike to discard any original parts, if we wish such pieces for daily use in our homes we may have to install new runs, this being an easily accomplished detail of restoration. If, however, our piece is a "show piece," more to be admired than to be used, we may leave the old runs in place and so save these worn and interesting structural parts.

The bottom edges of drawers, where they come into contact with the runs, are also frequently badly worn, but these may easily be repaired with a narrow strip of wood glued on and fastened with several wire brads driven through the strip into the worn edges.

THE RESTORATION OF CARVING

Unless we are somewhat familiar with carving, we shall be wise to retain the services of some professional if our work in restoring such details is at all complex. However, on some minor restoration of carved work, we may set in a piece of wood of suitable size and later carve it according to the old design. For some of this work plastic wood does very well, as it is strong, dries hard, and may be easily carved. I recently repaired with this material a very dilapidated cock pheasant in the crest of a mahogany looking-glass and he is now a rather convincing and presentable bird.

RESTORING VENEERS AND INLAYS

It is probable that about the only veneered furniture on

which we shall be called to make restorations will be of mahogany, walnut, or rosewood. If we collect veneered furniture, we shall note that it suffers greater harm from hard use, age, and dampness than does furniture constructed of solid wood. The veneer on all corners and skirts, and on the edges of drawers and feet, will often be found knicked and broken. The veneer on table tops will frequently be loosened and blistered from dampness or carelessness with hot cooking utensils. I have often seen, in old homes, a collection of growing plants in pots installed on a veneered table or chest of drawers. Such a use would, of course, in time be ruinous to any veneered piece.

As previously mentioned, we should not attempt to spend much money and time in restoring the more common type of veneered furniture, if it is in very bad condition. At the best, a much restored piece of veneered furniture will present a more or less patchwork effect and the common pieces are not worth the effort—they are too easily accessible in fairly good condition.

If we should be so lucky as to acquire a six-leg highboy of the vintage of 1710, we would be very willing to restore, to almost any degree, its lost or broken walnut veneer, but when we consider taking on a wrecked chest of drawers of the Victorian era, which has stood in a leaky barn until the thin veneer hangs loose like the bark of our native shagbark hickory tree, we shall do well to hesitate before making out the check.

The restoration of entire or extensive surfaces of veneer such as the top of a mahogany table will probably be rather too ambitious an operation for most amateurs. Small patches and knicks may be cut out so as to leave straight, sharp edges, and all old glue removed from the surface. Then bits of old veneer, cut to proper size, may be set in with glue and held in place a moment with a hot flatiron. The heat will quickly dry the glue and obviate all need of clamps.

The use of old veneer is recommended for these small repairs, as the color is dark and the surface is filled with old finish. New veneer, which is light in color and unfilled, will give us considerable trouble in coloring and finishing. However, we should see that the old veneer restoration is of the same thickness as is that of the piece we are treating, and that all old glue is scraped from its under surface. New glue anywhere applied over old glue does not adhere well. Very small breaks in veneer are often repaired by pressing in stick shellac of exactly the right shade with a hot iron as has been previously explained.

This does very well on flat surfaces, but stick shellac is brittle and, if used to replace veneer on the edges and corners of posts and drawers, is likely to chip out under everyday use. Plastic wood is preferable for such repairs, as it is much stronger and less brittle than stick shellac.

Veneered pieces often suffer, particularly on their tops, from blisters and waves, the result of dampness or the careless spilling of boiling water. These blisters look very much like those which appear on the hands of the amateur gardener who, after a winter of ease, decides in April to personally spade his entire vegetable patch. Sometimes they are broken, but often quite intact. If broken, dirt may have worked into them and so prevent their being glued again into a smooth surface. If the blisters *are* broken, we may work in some glue with a thin splinter of wood and hold down the loosened spot for a few moments with a rather hot flatiron.

If we find that the blister will not return to a level position, it is a sign that dirt has entered the break. In such a case we may try carefully cutting the veneer on three sides of the blister—two cuts being with the grain, one cut across the grain—lifting the flap thus created, scraping out the interfering dirt, and again gluing the flap of veneer into place. If the blister or wave is unbroken, and the cause of the upheaval was not a lack of glue, we may simply try standing a hot flatiron on the offending spot until the iron cools. There is always in all woods, unless kiln or oven dried, considerable water content, and the hot iron will sufficiently vaporize this moisture to dampen the old glue and firmly cement the blister in place.

INLAYS

If we except the marquetry of the early Dutch furniture, we shall find little use of true inlay in woods of contrasting colors until after the year 1725. From about this period we find an increasing use of inlay, the fashion reaching its height in the time of Hepplewhite and Sheraton, and decreasing in Empire and Victorian days. Various sorts of line inlay were in common use, as well as intricate and beautiful scrolls, fans, medallions, wreaths, garlands, and festoons of flowers.

Bands of inlay were employed on the edges of table tops and on drawers and legs—positions on which wear often brought about serious damage. We shall observe that inlaid furniture will often need a considerable amount of restoration. If any inlay has merely become loosened, it can easily be glued in place as we glue veneer; and, if line inlay is lost, we may purchase some and restore it. Tiny bits of lost one-color inlay may be filled in with stick shellac. But if some almost forgotten Aunt should bequeath to us a set of Hepplewhite inlaid dining tables, on which many pieces of the delicate flower inlay were lacking, we should not attempt personally to accomplish such restoration. Such work is only within the powers of the expert and specialist, as are other restorative processes such as elaborate carving, repairing plaster-work looking glasses, and the application of large areas of new veneer.

WINDSOR CHAIRS

The repair and restoration of Windsor Chairs are not easy operations. There is hardly a right angle anywhere in Windsor construction. Every part slants, diverges, converges, and curves. Every hole slants, and slants at just the proper angle to receive its concomitant part. In a Windsor armchair, every spindle not only slopes outward from the seat, but diverges from its neighbor. In the arm rail, the holes for the spindles must not only be put exactly in the right location, but must each be bored at the right angle to accommodate the diverging spindles. It is said that the old-time Windsor chair-makers accomplished most of their operations "by eye" and with no precisional aids. If this be true, I wish to state that the oft-told tales of our ancestors shooting squirrels through the eye with a Kentucky rifle, at three hundred yards, are easily to be accepted. When the amateur has made and placed in position his first complete new arm rail for a Windsor armchair, he will have become more familiar with these matters of which I write.

Windsor chairs of the best early types were commonly constructed of several different sorts of wood. The *seats* were usually of a single piece of *white pine, basswood*, or *tulipwood*; the *legs* and *stretchers of maple*; the *hoop*, or *bow*, of *white oak, hickory*, or *ash*. The light bent *arm rail* was of *oak, hickory*, or *ash*; the heavy sawn rail type of *maple*. The *spindles* were of *oak, hickory*, or *ash*, with a preference for hickory. The *comb* was of *oak, ash*, or *hickory*, as were the turned side spindles of fan-back Windsors. However, we cannot be too dogmatic about the materials which went into Windsor chairs, for many a variation will be found. A fine chair may have maple legs and oak stretchers. I have seen examples with legs and stretchers entirely of oak; and I own one fine fan-back side chair, which is, even including the seat, entirely of white oak. I have in my collection one armchair with a heavy chestnut seat, and I have seen several similar chairs with chestnut seats.

On most of the early Windsors the spindles were shaved out by hand. However, I possess several fine braced-back chairs of the best type, which have lathe-turned spindles; and we cannot say that no early Windsor ever has turned spindles. When we examine later Windsors the spindles are *nearly always* turned. The arm rails and bows and spindles of most early chairs are the evident result of the careful selection of very straight-grained wood and, secondly, of the use of drawknife, spokeshave, and small plane.

When we study the very late styles of Windsors—the so-called Sheraton Windsor, the square-back Windsor, the Windsor rocker, and the styles immediately preceding the Boston rocker, we shall note the predominance of maple throughout, except in the seats, which were of basswood, tulipwood, or pine.

OLD STRUCTURAL METHODS

The structure of fine Windsor chairs cannot but arouse our admiration. Here we find our strongest and most elastic woods combined in slender, sound, and graceful harmony of line and form. The seats and legs were made of green or unseasoned wood: the stretchers, bows, and spindles of seasoned wood. The stretchers were turned with slightly bulbous ends, which, after being driven into the holes bored for their reception, were held tightly by the shrinkage of the legs. It is probable that, at this point in the process, the underbody was left for a period, so that the legs would become dry before setting them with wedges into the green seat.

The spindles were dry, as was probably the bent bow. The lower ends of both the dry spindles and bow would be firmly held by the shrinkage of the green seat. On the arm chairs it is probable that the arm rail was put in place before being thoroughly seasoned. Possibly the comb, on comb-back and fan-back chairs, was so treated—although, in taking Windsor chairs apart, the combs seem to come loose very readily. This combination of dry parts held in place by the shrinkage of green parts would have been open to considerable variation according to the type of chair and the location of the parts. At any rate, the system was so well worked out that we find many Windsors which, after a century of use, are as sound and tight as when made.

SPINDLES, BOWS, AND COMBS

The spindles of Windsor chairs were often held by tiny wooden pins, or iron brads, inserted through the edges of the

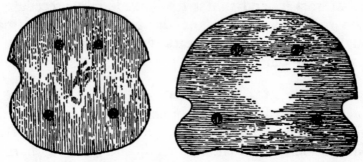

Fig. 12. Seats of Windsor Chairs with Wedged Leg-ends

seat. These pins and nails were also used on arm rails, bows, and combs to engage the spindles. We may be puzzled in attempting to re-glue a loose Windsor chair thus fastened, as there will be no way to remove the pins or nails without seriously disfiguring the wood. If such chairs are loose enough to have some "play," we may, as previously described, "work" or "rock" this glue into their joints without taking them apart.

GRAIN OF SEATS

Windsor side chairs were always made with the grain of the wood in the seat at right angles to the front of the seat.

In the arm types, with the exception of the one-piece-arm-and-back sort, the grain of the wood in the seat was parallel with the front of the seat. The legs of early Windsors usually entirely penetrate the seat and are wedged in place. Sometimes, and more often on the larger armchairs, the legs *do not* penetrate the seat or show on its upper surface. In this case, a straight-sided hole was bored into the under side of the seat, instead of the shapely tapered hole employed when the leg was intended completely to penetrate the seat. The end of the leg was then sawed, and a fox-tail wedge of proper thickness lightly inserted into the cut. When the leg was driven into the hole, the wedge, coming into contact with the end of the boring, forced the wedge home, spread the end of the leg and produced a tight joint.

WEDGED LEGS

Whenever Windsor chairs were wedged, either at the top of the legs on the ends of the bow underneath the seat, or

Fig. 13. Wedges of Windsor Chair Legs

at the top and bottom of the under-arm spindles, the wedges were always set at right angles to the grain of the wood which the wedged member engaged. In this way a terrific pressure could be produced without danger of splitting. The wedges of Windsors were sometimes of the same slanting thickness throughout, but we often find wedges cut, apparently with intention, wider on one side and with a sharp corner on this wide side. Such a wedge would not only spread the sawed section, but would, when driven, be forced

in a lateral direction, causing the acute corner to bite deeply
into the surrounding wood.

CLEAN BREAKS

Windsor chairs come to us in various states of disrepair—
spindles, combs, one or more legs or stretchers missing,
arm rails or bows broken. Bad breaks in Windsor chairs are
most often found in four spots: namely, at the ends of the
back bow close to the seat; where the spindles are set into
the bow; at the section of the arm rail where a mortise was
cut to receive the tenon on the end of the top bow; and at
the sharp bend at the back of the arm of the one-piece-arm-
and-back chair. In the first three instances, weakness was
due to an unavoidable cutting of the wood which caused
an inevitable break under strain at these weakened points.
If, in any of these locations, the wood is broken squarely
off, a permanent repair is difficult to accomplish. We may, if
we consider ourselves sufficiently dexterous, "halve in" new
sections of wood to replace the broken sections; but we must
allow enough space to make a proper and carefully fitted
joint, glued and held by small screws. If the break is a
slanting one, it may be glued in place and likewise held by
small screws. Spindles are often broken off squarely, immediately under the bow. These may be repaired by carefully
drilling a small hole from the top of the bow through the
piece of spindle remaining in the hole and about two inches
into the top of the broken spindle. A small finishing nail
of the same diameter and height as the hole may be inserted,
along with a drop of glue. We should not try to drive the
nail beyond the length of the drilled hole, or a split spindle
will surely result.

NEW WOOD FOR REPAIRS

Old wood is dry and brittle and is of no use for any parts
of Windsor chairs which must be steamed and bent. For

such work we must have *new* wood. If we wish to make any important restorations on Windsor chairs, we should have some pieces of new, sound, very straight-grained hickory, white oak, and ash, absolutely free of knots, and of these dimensions, in inches: 72 x 1 square, 72 x ⅞ square, 72 x ⅞ x 2, 24 x 1 x 3.

With these sizes in the woods stipulated, we are ready to match the old woods commonly employed in the steamed and bent parts of Windsors. The 72-inch x 1-inch square material will be correct for any bow. The 72-inch x ⅞-inch square material will be correct for lighter bows and the largest spindles. The 72-inch x ⅞-inch x 2-inch material will be for arm rails where the section to be bent is cut down to one-inch square before steaming and bending; while the 2-inch width allows for the front arm ends. The 24-inch x 1-inch x 3-inch material is for combs.

NEW SPINDLES

Windsor chair spindles are of various patterns, but all the early sorts are tapered both ways and some show a rather pronounced bulb. They may be made from the ⅞-square material by working them into rough form with a draw-knife and later finishing them with a small spokeshave and a very small plane.

When the drawknife and spokeshave are used, the spindle may be held in a vice.

When the *plane* is employed, I drive a small wire nail about a foot from the edge of the workbench, with the head about one-quarter of an inch above the surface. The spindle is held by the outer end in the left hand, the opposite end being pushed firmly against the sharp edge of the nail, and the spindle held at a right angle to the front edge of the bench. Thus, 12 inches of spindle lies on the bench, the remaining length being unsupported except by the left hand. A slight downward pressure with the left hand enables the spindle to be curved and sprung at will. And with a small, short, and very sharp plane, the spindle may be quickly brought to any desired pattern and shape. Springing the spindle as we work, allows us to leave curved surfaces which could otherwise be obtained only by the use of a spokeshave.

STEAMING AND BENDING

If we wish to produce bows, arm rails or combs, we must have some means of steaming the wood. I use a home-made

Fig. 14.   Making a New Bow for a Windsor Chair

affair which works very well for a limited amount of this work. The device is simply a six-foot section of galvanized leader pipe, four inches in diameter, with a cap soldered over one end. This is filled with water, the capped end placed in a fire, and the pieces to be steamed are thrust into the open end and allowed to simmer for three or four hours. The four-inch diameter of the pipe is adequate in size for any piece of wood we shall wish to steam.

The old-time Windsor makers, who produced quantities of chairs, had forms in various sizes of wood or metal to which they clamped the steamed wood. But, in restoring Windsors, almost every chair will be of individual size and shape, and we cannot have heavy forms of all sizes on hand.

My system of forming bows, arm rails and combs, where only one of its kind is wanted, is shown in the accompanying drawings. The section to be bent should first be planed down almost to its final size, leaving only enough wood to allow for removing edges and the inevitable roughness that comes from steaming and drying. .

In planning to make a bow, we first cut a paper pattern of the exact outside shape of bow we desire, and, with a few tacks, fasten this paper onto the top of a strong wide work-

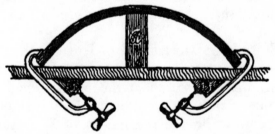

Fig. 15.   Making a Comb for a Windsor Chair

bench or table. A curved block, one and one-quarter inches in thickness, is fastened with screws at point A, far enough below the edge of the pattern to allow for the thickness of the bow. Additional blocks are then set at various points outside the edge of the paper pattern, the number and position of the blocks being somewhat influenced by the size and shape of the piece we wish to bend.

The bow having been planed down almost to its final size, has been steamed for several hours, until it is soft and pliable. The straight piece is first clamped with a strong clamp at figure A of the drawing. Then, proceeding around the edge of the pattern the bow is bent within the blocks and fastened with clamps. It should be left for several days to become thoroughly dry before the clamps are removed. By this system we can produce any form of bow or arm rail.

A comb of any desired length or degree of curvature may be made as shown in Figure 15. A strong block *A* of length sufficient to give the desired curvature is nailed upright at the edge of a strong bench. Triangular blocks *BB* are nailed on the under side of the bench so that the clamps may obtain a straight pull on the ends of the steamed and bent comb.

In making a comb, it is best to do the work of rounding the ends, and thinning and shaping the upper edge, *after* the comb is bent and thoroughly dry. In boring the holes in rails, bows, and combs, we should see that our auger bits are exceedingly sharp, so that we may produce clean, smooth holes.

If Windsor chairs are lacking in legs or stretchers, these may be turned from old maple; and remember that, if the original turnings are scored at the points where holes are bored, the new turnings should be similarly marked.

To the beginner in the restoration of Windsor chairs, I would say, Do not become discouraged if your first efforts seem rather unsuccessful. Most of the methods and processes employed on Windsors are very different from regular cabinetwork. Even expert cabinetmakers, sometimes, are not at all successful when they attempt to treat wrecked Windsor chairs. I frankly acknowledge that some of my own early efforts in restoring Windsors, appeared very much as might those of the manual training department of a summer camp for small boys.

ALL RESTORATIONS COMPLETE

All restorations should be quite finished and complete before any attempt is made to clean off the old piece. All joints will be smooth and even, all sharp edges and corners will have been removed, the piece will be sound and whole, and in such a condition that no further cutting, planing, or sawing operations are needed. If every detail of restoration is completed before the piece is cleaned off, this final operation will at least partially stain the new sections with the color of the old finish, and more or less bring them into harmony of color and tone with the original parts.

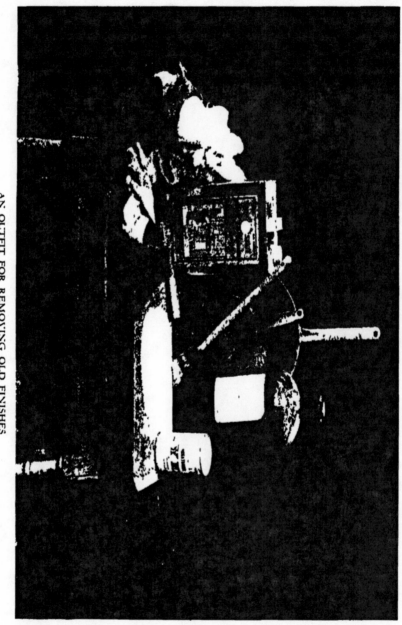

PLATE 15

AN OUTFIT FOR REMOVING OLD FINISHES

Varnish-remover, lye, savogran, alcohol, pans, paint-brush, scrubbing-brush, dish-mop rubber gloves, cloth, and burlap

Chapter VI

REMOVING OLD FINISHES AND PREPARING
FOR NEW ONES

WHEN we reach the point of removing old finishes from our early furniture, we must first consider *whether or not we really do want to remove them.* We shall, of course, find some pieces which have had one, or many, coats of varnish—now possibly cracked and stained. But, in such cases, cleaning and smoothing are easy. Sometimes we may find furniture of light-colored wood, such as maple or pine, which has been deeply stained in imitation of mahogany. Such examples are extremely hard to restore to anything like their proper color: probably only after thorough scraping can the desired result be accomplished. Perhaps we shall find a certain number of pieces which are original and intact in every way, and still have their original coats of finish.

REFINISHING NOT ALWAYS DESIRABLE

In mahogany, walnut, or maple, we may occasionally find a piece intact and with its original varnish well preserved, and with a smooth surface mellowed by time to a delightful patina. It is considered to be in the best taste to retain such a piece "as is," except for a good rubbing with brown wax (as later described) or with furniture polish.

In painted furniture, we must distinguish between an original finish—which is likely to be merely a single coat of red, dark green, gray, or black paint—and superimposed finishes, which may consist of from two to fifteen coats of old paint and varnish put on at irregular periods during the career of the piece.

If we can find a piece carrying its first single coat of paint

83

and wish to keep it as found, we need only to wash it gently with soap and water, and, when dry, rub it well with brown wax or furniture polish. Washing will remove the old grime; the wax or polish will sufficiently restore the color, and will give a dull gloss.

PAINTED MAHOGANY

We may find pieces of furniture, either solid or veneered, overlaid with successive coats of many sorts of varnish, paint, and varnish stains. It is rather a mystery why anyone should ever have wished to apply paint to the surface of fine old mahogany, cherry, or walnut furniture. But, whatever the reason, such treatment was quite common. Only recently I saw a handsome inlaid mahogany sideboard whose beauty had been thoroughly concealed by a heavy coat of brown paint.

Any mahogany, cherry, or walnut piece which has been painted white (a not uncommon treatment) is very difficult to clean, as the white paint enters into every pore and crack, and, even after cleaning, is likely to show in violent contrast with the darker original wood. As one refinisher, almost without exaggeration, remarked, "The only thing to do is to pick out the white with a pin." A piece made of dark wood which has been painted brown, or red, is not nearly so difficult to bring into a proper state of cleanness.

AVOID THE SCRAPER

Let me next observe that a knife, a scraper, or pieces of broken glass should play as little part as possible in cleaning old furniture, glass is dangerous to the user and bad for any furniture. We often hear the expression "scraping down," in connection with old furniture, which usually means the avoidance of varnish remover, or other solvents, and the use of scrapers or knives for removing overlays of paints and varnish. Such harsh treatment takes off not only the old finish, but also the outer surface of the wood, *which*

PLATE 16

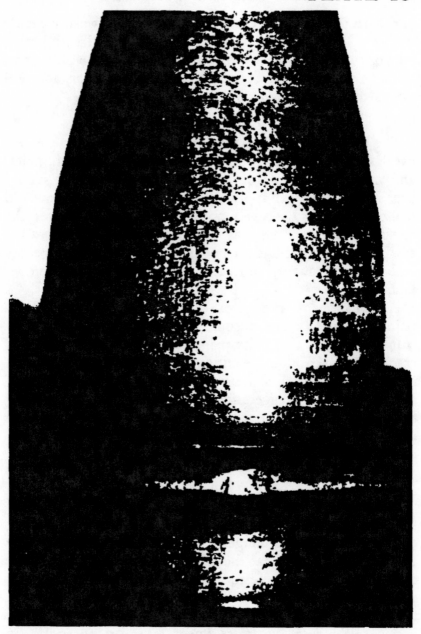

MARKS OF THE TURNER'S CHISEL ON A WINDSOR CHAIR-LEG
These should be preserved to show authenticity

above everything we want to save. Particularly harmful is the scraping down of any turning, such as that of a Windsor chair leg. Since much pressure must be used in this process, the scraper moves irregularly over the surface of the turning and leaves, inevitably, a rough, scarred and jagged member.

Modern turning-lathes have a speed of from two thousand to five thousand revolutions per minute, and sandpaper is used to smooth the revolving wood. Old turning-lathes ran slowly and when the turner's curved chisel progressed bit by bit over the gradually revolving surface of a Windsor chair leg, or the leg of a tavern table, it left shallow spiral grooves running about the leg. The plane was the tool used by old-time joiners for smoothing. Until rather a late date, sandpaper was not known. The old planes had a blade with a slightly curved edge, so that each stroke left in the surface of the wood a wide, shallow, slightly rounded track. These plane marks may often be seen on chest ends, drawer fronts, and table frames. All these marks of the turner's chisel and the joiner's place are valuable evidences of old, slow, honest work, and are nearly always to be found either on the exterior or the interior surfaces of our early furniture. They are almost never found on reproductions. The removal of these traces renders the piece thus treated just so much the less desirable. *Deeply scraping down early furniture is quite as bad, and quite as disastrous, as buffing early silver and pewter,* or allowing fine old oil portraits to be "touched up" by some helpful, but inexpert, "artistic" friend.

SOLVENTS FOR OLD FINISHES

When we are ready to clean our old furniture, whether entirely original or restored, there are three solvents whose uses we may consider: *varnish remover, lye,* and *savogran.*

These three solvents are fiery compounds, and should be used with care and kept away from the user's eyes. A pair of thin rubber gloves save the hands; and old clothing should be worn while any cleaning-off is being done. Lye, particularly, will remove not only paint, but the soles of shoes, finger nails, sections of skin, and trouser legs as well.

Outdoors on bright and windy days these three solvents dry so quickly as to be of slight avail. They may, however, be used in the open in dull, damp, and still weather.

VARNISH REMOVER

Varnish remover is marketed under a number of different trade marks; but, as it is all made under the same patents, its composition and effect are virtually uniform. It comes in quart and gallon cans, and costs about three dollars per gallon.

Since varnish remover is very inflammable, its use near fire is to be avoided. Furthermore, when it is used in a small, closed room, its fumes will sometimes cause severe headache. It is rather slow in action and is expensive, but it is really our *best* solvent, as it does not injure the wood, raise the grain, or harm the glue. It leaves an entirely cleaned piece in fine condition for smoothing.

Its action is particularly slow on old, thick, and hard paints; but comparatively rapid on one or two coats of varnish or varnish stain. If, for instance, we are cleaning an old Windsor chair which carries five or six coats of flinty paint, we might easily use an entire gallon of remover, at three dollars, where one can of lye at fifteen cents would do the same work more quickly. Where glued restorations have been necessary, or on any veneered furniture, varnish remover does not loosen or dissolve the glue. Lye and savogran on the other hand, because of their water content, will often produce just that unfortunate result. *Varnish remover is positively the only solvent suitable for use on veneered furniture, and experimentation with lye or savogran on veneers will bring only disastrous results.*

Apply varnish remover with an old two-inch or three-inch

PLATE 17

PLANE MARKS ON PINE DRAWER BOTTOM OF A CHEST OF ABOUT 1750
Such marks are not found on reproductions

brush, daubing the liquid thoroughly over the entire surface of the piece. Within fifteen minutes or half an hour the surface of the old finish will be softened, and we may remove it with a dull putty knife. For wiping-off turned sections, pieces of rough old burlap work well. Successive coats of varnish remover, followed by the use of the dull putty knife and burlap, will eventually remove most of the old paint or finish.

When almost all of the old paint has been taken off, we may try rubbing the piece with fine steel wool while the remover is still moist. This often works very well in removing obstinate colors from flat surfaces and turnings.

A clean brush and fresh varnish remover are now used for a final thorough application which, in turn, is wiped off with clean burlap. The piece may now be wiped with a soft cloth soaked in wood- or denatured-alcohol, which should do away with almost all of the last traces of color and remover. This alcohol bath will sometimes produce on mahogany, after drying, a queer milky surface; but this is nothing to disturb us, as it will quickly disappear during the smoothing with fine sandpaper or steel wool.

A piece covered with but a single coat of paint or varnish may be cleaned with one or two applications of the remover, but those carrying many coats of hard paint or old varnish may require as many as a dozen or more applications.

WHEN TO SHELLAC

No move toward shellacking any piece which has been cleaned with varnish remover should be made *under twenty-four hours*, as this period allows the last traces of the remover to evaporate. Shellac applied too soon over traces of remover may later become white and discolored.

Whatever solvent is used in cleaning furniture, great care should be taken to avoid spilling it about on the interiors of drawers or on any surface that was not originally finished.

All drawers should be removed, and a separate operation made of cleaning them.

The back of any cabinet piece should be slightly elevated with blocks, so that the front is not perpendicular, but tips forward. This tilt will prevent any of the remover or solvent from running, or oozing, into the vacant drawer openings. The interiors and backs of genuine cabinet pieces, all the surface of drawers, and the under side of table tops have a fine, distinctive old-brown color, which only age can produce. Any of the solvent mixed with finish and carelessly spilled over these beautiful surfaces seriously detracts from their appearance. The inside sections of a fine old cabinet piece are almost as interesting to an expert collector as are its outer surfaces.

LYE

Lye is a powerful, corrosive chemical, selling in most grocery stores at fifteen cents per can. Its action, when mixed with water, is very rapid, and it is the cheapest available solvent. *I should hesitate to advise any general use of lye in cleaning furniture, as it has a way of entering deeply into soft, porous woods, sometimes discoloring and darkening them, and later working out through the final finish of shellac and wax, eventually turning them white.*

Very strong lye will burn wood and cause the surfaces of turnings, when dry, to show hundreds of small longitudinal cracks. Its destructive power will be demonstrated if we immerse a small block of wood in a strong solution for a few days. By the end of that time the wood will be reduced to a slimy pulp. I have done considerable experimenting with the use of lye as a solvent, and have found it *least harmful* to maple, hickory, and pine. I have used it on very heavily painted Windsor chairs and tavern tables with not bad results. I have also used it, at times, for *starting* the outer coats of paint on heavily painted furniture.

It would probably be sound advice to say, *never* use lye on oak, walnut, chestnut, and butternut, or other more or less porous open-grained woods. It should *never* be used on cherry, which it turns to a sickly reddish drab, and *certainly not* on mahogany, which it quite ruins.

If we decide to try lye on a heavily painted piece of furniture, let the solution be not too strong, and the piece not too valuable. I have used lye on many different pieces, and expect to continue to do so; but I hesitate to recommend its general use for this reason: with varnish remover the amateur can do little damage to any piece; while with lye, improperly applied, he may accomplish a good deal of permanent harm.

Bearing these warnings in mind, the beginner will probably do well to avoid the use of lye. But if he wishes to experiment, here is the method:

Lye may be mixed with warm water in varying strengths; from one-eighth to one-half can of lye to one gallon of water. It cannot be applied with a brush, as it quickly destroys the bristles. The solution may best be put on with a wooden-handled cotton dishmop, such as may be purchased for ten cents. It may be dabbled about on the painted surfaces so as to keep them constantly moist. If this mop is occasionally rubbed in ordinary garden soil, the grit will help abrade the loosened paint.

The low price of lye allows its free use without much regard to economy, which must be considered when we are employing the much more expensive varnish removers.

Lye mixed with water enters deeply into wood, and leaves a wet shiny film, which should be removed with a scrubbing brush and clear water. Any piece cleaned with lye should be scrubbed, *over and over again,* to bring forth every particle of the chemical from the cracks, joints, seams, and pores of the wood. Any lack of thoroughness in washing with much clear water will later cause trouble under the final finish. I have seen lye carelessly applied to old chests with a broom, and later washed with a hose, much to the detriment of the inner surfaces. Improbable as the statement may seem, a garden hose will *not* properly remove the film which comes with the use of lye.

As has been warned, lye raises the grain of wood and leaves a much rougher surface than does varnish remover; but it does pull refractory paints and stains out of the pores of the wood much more successfully than does the remover. After using varnish remover for hours on some particularly mean and tenacious coat of old red paint, I have, at times, lost patience and descended to the use of lye. It will certainly start old paint as will nothing else.

SAVOGRAN

Savogran is a fine, white powder, obtainable at most paint stores at about fifteen cents per pound. Its action, when mixed with water, is much slower than that of lye; it is not so corrosive, and is not so harmful to hands and clothing. It has an advantage over lye in that it does not enter so deeply into the wood, nor so thoroughly raise and roughen surfaces. It has the same power as lye to enter into the pores of wood and to loosen and bring forth old paints and stains. Savogran will leave surfaces in better condition than lye, but not in so good condition as varnish remover. Savogran, like lye, is slow in action, and any piece could probably be cleaned off more quickly with varnish remover than with savogran. Its cheapness is its chief recommendation.

The correct solution strength of savogran is from one quarter pound to one pound mixed with one gallon of *hot* water, as it dissolves more quickly in hot water. It should be *applied only when cool.* A weak solution of savogran may be used in place of alcohol, after a piece is cleaned with varnish remover, to wash off the last traces of the remover and paints.

PLATE 18

A UNDER SIDE OF MAPLE TABLE WITH TRACES OF AUTHENTIC OLD PAINT

B SCORING-MARKS ON OLD CHAIR-POSTS

Note how these are almost obliterated by the wear of shoulders at the second slat

Savogran may safely be employed by the amateur or inexperienced finisher on any solid furniture of native woods except cherry—which it seems to discolor. He cannot seriously damage either his furniture or himself with this solvent. It should *never* be used on any veneered furniture, or on mahogany.

Savogran may be applied like lye, with a cotton dishmop, or with a bristle paint brush. Bristles are not injured by savogran. The directions for applying lye may be followed in the case of savogran. In the end, the piece of furniture should be very thoroughly washed and scrubbed with plenty of clean water before being put away to dry.

Savogran will leave any piece on which it is used very light in color, as it has strong bleaching powers.

LEAVE SOME TRACES OF PAINT

Whatever solvents we use, let us not be over-particular in removing the last traces of old paint from certain parts of our furniture. In the deep turnings of Windsor chair legs and the legs of turned tables, a slight trace of red, green, or black paint is attractive and indicates authenticity. A bit of old paint left on the under side of table tops, outside the frame, does not show when the table has been refinished and is in use; yet, if the table is turned over for close examination, this old paint will give a comfortable assurance of age.

REMOVING STAINS AND FILLING CAVITIES

Often we shall find table tops or the interior parts of desks badly stained with black or red ink. Ink stains penetrate deeply into the wood, but these and other stains may be minimized by applications of pure ammonia, or a saturated solution of oxalic acid. The spots so treated should, after drying, be rubbed smooth with steel wool.

Sometimes solid wood furniture will have acquired deep dents. These may be treated by placing three or four thicknesses of damp cloth over the dent and applying a hot flat-iron. The steam and heat will soften, swell, and raise the crushed fibre, tending to correct the trouble.

After cleaning our furniture we may find bad nail or knot holes, cracks, or places which require filling. Tiny bits of veneer may be missing. Stick shellac or plastic wood may be used for this filling, as described in a previous chapter. When varnish remover is to be used as a solvent the filling of these cavities should previously be accomplished. If lye or savogran be used, the filling should be done *after* the finish is removed, as the water content of these solvents tends to wash out and displace the filling.

SMOOTHING

Our furniture, at this point, needs smoothing—a treatment which will bring all its surfaces to a fine, silky condition without obliterating the interesting evidences of age and use. So we arrive at the question of suitable abrasives. We should remember that the purpose of abrasives of any sort on antique furniture is for *smoothing* and not for *scratching*. We are not removing rust from old ironwork, or preparing to paint a house, operations where the use of coarse sandpaper is indicated and proper. *We are working on fine old surfaces which we wish to smooth without leaving any after-traces or marks of abrasives.*

Of these, the only two worth consideration are *sandpaper* and *steel wool*. Many finishers depend entirely on sandpaper, often of the coarser grades only. In ignoring the aid of steel wool, they lose a valuable ally.

Sandpaper comes in many degrees of coarseness, and may be purchased at any paint store. The better grades are made of a very tough paper, and are lasting and economical. These are my recommendations as to sandpaper surfaces:

Number 2 sandpaper is too coarse for favorable use on furniture. Number 1 sandpaper might, at times, be used, as on a very rough table top, but it is somewhat too coarse. Number 1/2 sandpaper is a better grade for any rough operation.

The sizes of sandpaper on which we shall depend for most of our work are Number 1/o, Number 2/o, and Number 3/o.

In using, we should always (except, perhaps, with the finest grades) rub *with* the grain of the wood. Coarse sandpaper used *across* the grain badly scratches and mars the surface. Indeed a single energetic rub across the grain of a fine mahogany table top with Number 2 sandpaper will so mar it that a scraper will be required to remove the damage.

Coarse grades naturally do their work very quickly; hence their common use, and hence the frequent sight of old furniture full of unpleasant marks and scratches under the final finish. All such marks are accentuated, just as the grain of wood is emphasized, when the shellac is applied. A piece which appears to be nicely smoothed may, after shellacking, exhibit very apparent marks of sandpaper or a dull nicked scraper. *We should always remember that there is absolutely no danger of making any piece too smooth.*

In smoothing we may first use the relatively coarse grades of sandpaper and afterward the finer ones. If ever in doubt, we may safely incline toward the finer grades. Much rubbing with these latter will produce beautiful results; a little rubbing with only the coarse sizes will work quite otherwise.

Sandpaper, being brittle and tearable, does not work well on turnings, where a sheet will go to pieces quickly. *Emery cloth,* similar to sandpaper except that it has a backing of cloth instead of paper, is useful on deep turnings, and one sheet of it will outlast many of sandpaper. The finer grades, of course, should be used.

Steel wool is to be found at paint and hardware stores in one-quarter, one-half, and one pound packages, priced according to grades. Number 1 is the coarsest grade that we shall require for our furniture. Number o is a finer type, and the one we shall most commonly use. Number oo is extremely fine and soft, and may be employed for a final rubbing, if we want extreme smoothness.

Steel wool is used in small handfuls. An old leather glove should be worn during its application. If a glove is not worn, particles of steel wool will sometimes work into the hand, like splinters, making spots which become extremely sore. Steel wool in use disintegrates into millions of tiny particles, and, therefore, should not be used outdoors when the wind is blowing, on account of the danger of its getting into the eyes.

It works well on flat surfaces that are not too rough or splintery. A handful worked up and down and around a turning, gives a fine smooth finish. The leg of a Windsor chair can be properly smoothed with steel wool in half the time required with sandpaper. Fine steel wool does not, in any way, impair the marks of the turner's chisel on old turnings, nor the plane marks on flat surfaces. *The finer grades may be worked in any direction, either with or across the grain; it leaves no scratches.*

Steel wool works best on the harder woods, and not so well on soft woods, if they are at all rough. Such surfaces may best be smoothed with fine sandpaper. On maple, and on solid or veneered mahogany, a persistent rubbing with steel wool brings a surface that is the perfection of smoothness. It is an ideal abrasive for the use of the amateur finisher. He may rub to his heart's content, knowing that the more he rubs the finer will be the surface of his furniture.

THE CABINET SCRAPER

Occasionally, on flat surfaces which are badly stained, the help of a cabinet scraper will be needed. If this be used at all, it should be very sharp, and should be lightly handled, not with the intention of deeply removing the surface of

PLATE 19

LOWER CORNER OF A TURNED BUTTERFLY TABLE

Though refinished, this retains marks of turner's chisel, old paint,
wear and evidence of age An unwise use of scraper and sand paper
would have obliterated these guarantees of authenticity

Chapter VII

REFINISHING

IF THE directions and suggestions of previous chapters have been carefully followed, our furniture, at this point, will be ready for its final finish.

Some woods, such as tulipwood, maple, oak and pine, are subject to borers and worms. Mahagony and walnut are fairly immune from such attacks. Even after the refinishing process, these pests will sometimes continue to work, and will daily thrust out fine wood dust from the entrances of their homes. They may be killed by a thorough soaking with gasoline, which evaporates quickly and in no way harms the wood.

If our furniture is of solid mahogany, rosewood, or Victorian walnut, or if it is veneered, it was not originally intended to be painted and so should show no traces of paint anywhere. But if it be of the type of early Windsor chairs, tavern tables, or softwood cupboards, which were nearly always painted, a few traces of the old paint may be allowed to remain about the pins, in cracks and joints, or in the deep parts of turnings.

If restorations have been necessary it will be remembered that the restored parts will probably appear lighter in color than the original surfaces. *Something must now be done to bring these restored parts to a color harmonizing with the old surfaces.*

TOUCHING UP THE NEW WITH COLOR

For this work, nothing is more satisfactory than the decorators' oil colors, which come in tubes and may be purchased at most paint stores and from dealers in artists' supplies. If we have on hand a tube each of *burnt umber, chrome green,*

PLATE 20

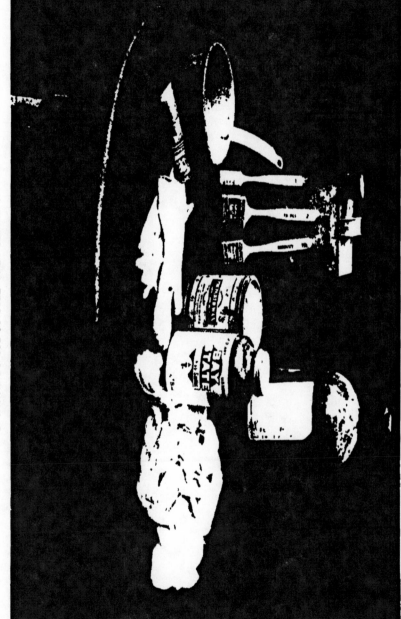

AN OUTFIT OF MATERIALS FOR REFINISHING

black, white, Indian red, chrome yellow, dark blue, and *dark mahogany,* we may, by using the pure colors, closely approximate the old surface tones of any piece, whether solid or veneered.

If, for instance, we are working on a Windsor chair whose feet have been restored, we first moisten the feet with a little linseed oil. Then, with the hand or a bit of rag we shall work in just enough of the burnt umber to match the color of the old maple legs. If the maple shows traces of red stains or paint, we may also apply to each foot a tiny fleck of Indian red, worked into the first coat of burnt umber.

The quantity of color required for such work is *very* small. By careful experiment and blending, we may hit very well the old shades. If our efforts are not at first successful, we may wipe off the application with linseed oil and try again. This work is interesting and gives us opportunity to test the accuracy of our color sense.

If we have been forced to restore any large surfaces with new wood of light color, such as pine or tulipwood table tops or drawer fronts, they are not easily brought to a plausible appearance of antiquity. They are, of course, to begin with, absolutely smooth and unmarred. We do not want artificially to mar, scratch, and dent these new surfaces, as is sometimes done, for such work borders too closely on the illegitimate. We may darken these new surfaces with walnut stain much diluted with turpentine and attain any desired shade of brown, but the effect will still be new. After all this has been done, we shall probably wish that we had taken the trouble to find *old wood* for the restorations, and vow to do so on the next piece to be treated.

After the restored sections have been brought to a suitably harmonious color, the piece should be put aside for twenty-four hours to dry.

This staining or coloring of restored parts is quite proper, and is not "faking." It is done so that, when the finished furniture is placed in our homes, there need be no shocking or violent variations in color. We need not fear that our effort to obtain harmonious color will in any way confuse the expert. If restorations have been made, a careful examination will quickly disclose them, no matter how successfully colored they may be.

The question whether it is desirable to stain maple, pine, or tulipwood to simulate mahogany sometimes arises. Such staining would seem to be poor practice. There is one place where it might be permissible. When we want a room entirely furnished in mahogany, it is very difficult to find a mahogany bed at any reasonable price; hence many collectors meet their requirements by staining mahogany one of the handsomely turned low-post maple beds of the 1840's and 50's.

If we wish to use a mahogany stain, let us be particular that it is the very dark brownish-red *oil* stain; not the gaudy bright red so prevalent at paint stores, or the *alcohol* stains, which are difficult to apply smoothly. Oil stain should be applied according to the directions on the can, after the old finish has been removed and the piece thoroughly smoothed. The surplus stain should be wiped off with a soft cloth before it has completely dried. If this is not done, the work is likely to be a patchy and uneven color.

Under no circumstances stain any fine maple bureaux, high-post beds, Windsor chairs, early gate-leg or tavern tables to imitate mahogany. Persons have been summarily executed for lesser crimes.

GENERAL-PURPOSE FINISH

We are now ready to proceed and shall first apply what I shall call our general-purpose finish. If we are dealing with expansive surfaces of new woods, we shall have to use some paste filler to close its pores. As most of our work will be on old woods, which have previously been painted and finished in various ways, the old surface pores are fairly well sealed, so no paste filler is required.

SHELLAC

Here *shellac* enters into our calculations. If we want to keep our furniture very light in color, we may use white shellac. I prefer and generally use the so-called orange, or brown, shellac, concerning which there seems to be considerable confusion—labels appearing to mean little. We find under the label of orange shellac various colors, from a gaudy orange which we must avoid, to a brown shade which is just what we want.

Therefore, see to it that, disregarding labels, we purchase a brown or brownish shade of shellac of the best grade and not the brilliant orange tint.

Shellac dries very quickly, and clear, heavy shellac is rather difficult to apply smoothly, especially around chair rungs and turnings. Moreover, we do not want a thick or heavy coat of shellac, or of anything else, on our early American furniture. Nothing could be in worse taste on such pieces than several heavy coats of varnish rubbed to a "piano" finish, although such modern treatment of early furniture is common.

It is only reasonable to allow that the finer and later types of mahogany and veneered furniture will submit more gracefully to such treatment than do the earlier and cruder styles. However, no piece of old furniture of any type or style should have such a varnished and shining surface as to reflect like a mirror the pained and startled countenance of the antique-lover who is closely inspecting it.

All that we require is a coating that will thoroughly seal the pores of the wood and offer a smooth surface and foundation for the application of our special brown wax, which is almost the last step in our finishing operations.

So we shall mix equal parts of wood- or denatured-alcohol with our white or orange shellac. White shellac should *not* be used on mahogany, walnut, or rosewood. This mixture will seem rather thin, but that is exactly what is needed. It should be applied very quickly with a fairly stiff brush; and, when applied about chair rungs or turnings, only in small brushfuls. By going over all surfaces two, three, or four times with this mixture, working very briskly and brushing until the brush is almost dry, we may produce a very fine, smooth surface, with no daubs, runs, or smears such as are likely to occur with the use of undiluted heavy shellac.

Soft, porous woods, such as pine, will absorb a much larger amount of shellac than will the harder woods like maple and cherry. Pine may need four coats of this thin mixture, while hard maple or mahogany may require but two. At any rate, we do not have to wait long for the coats to dry. This diluted shellac evaporates so quickly that by the time we have finished the last side of a chest of drawers the first side is dry enough to take on another coat. There is no waiting, as between successive coats of varnish. But we must remember that we want a sufficient shellac foundation so that our wax will have a surface on which to shine. For flat surfaces of mahogany, or any fine, hard wood on which a particularly smooth and even surface is desired, we may, when each successive coat of shellac is dry, give a light rubbing with very fine sandpaper or steel wool. But this procedure for any ordinary purpose is unnecessary.

After this shellac is smoothly and properly applied, the piece will show quite a sheen, even before the wax is used. Having thus thoroughly sealed the pores of the wood and prepared a smooth foundation, we shall find that our furniture is ready for its first coat of special brown wax.

WAX AND WAXING

Were we to use on our furniture any of the light yellow waxes, such as floor wax, we should find that, after the wax had dried, it would show almost white in cracks and joints. There are on the market a variety of so-called black waxes, made by mixing yellow wax and lampblack, and these are sometimes used on furniture. On dark woods, like mahogany and walnut, they are fairly satisfactory, but brown wax is better. They are not suitable for maple, pine, and light woods, to which their use imparts an unpleasant gray cast. Most of our furniture, when finished, should appear in various shades of warm browns and yellows, or, if of mahogany, reddish browns, and we want no gray or blackish effects if they can be avoided.

What we desire is a brown wax, and, so far as I know, the only way to obtain it is to prepare it ourselves. The market offers a number of reliable brands of yellow floor wax. These are combinations of paraffin, coloring matter, and alcohol or ether. They contain no beeswax and are known as "paraffin-base waxes."

We may place the contents of a pound can of yellow floor wax on a wide, smooth board, or table top; and, with a spatula or putty knife, thoroughly work into the wax a small level teaspoonful of burnt umber decorator's color. The wax may now be returned to the can, and we shall have a fine, brown tone wax, which may be used on early American furniture of every sort and color. It does not dry white, which is very important.

This wax is very inflammable; therefore we should not attempt to melt it on a stove and then mix the color with it. One of my friends once tried this method. After the fire department had extinguished the resulting conflagration, the cost of refinishing his kitchen was about seventy-five dollars.

With a soft cloth we may apply a thorough coat of the brown wax, working it well into the wood and covering all the thinly shellacked surfaces. We should do this work so that all the surfaces are covered by a fairly heavy coat of the moist wax, and we must see that no lumps are left in deep turnings or around chair rungs and stretchers. The piece may now be put aside in a warm room for twenty-four hours, after which it should be polished with an old soft woolen or cotton cloth. This process of waxing and rubbing may be repeated until three or four coats of brown wax have been used. Between the successive coats of wax, the piece should be left in a warm room, as wax dries very slowly in a low temperature.

A piece coated with brown wax and exposed to direct sunlight in warm weather dries within a few hours and is sooner ready for its rubbing, polish, and subsequent coat of wax.

The number of coats to be used may be determined, in any instance, by the hardness of the piece and by the degree of polish we wish to obtain. Each successive coat of well-rubbed wax will bring a richer lustre.

THIS FINISH ANSWERS ALL GENERAL PURPOSES

This general-purpose finish is the process I have used on virtually all the refinished furniture in my own collection, and I have found it most satisfactory. It gives a thin, smooth, and refined finish, showing pleasing high lights on turnings. It has no appearance of thickness or daubiness. It is not brittle, and it does not mar, chip, or bruise.

The whole process of applying this finish is simple, and I think the amateur finisher will do well to use it on all his furniture.

It has been employed on oak, walnut, cherry, pine, tulipwood, ash, butternut, sycamore, beech, maple, birch, and other native woods. It seems to work well on either soft or hard woods, and on woods of open or close grains. It is very satisfactory on mahogany and rosewood furniture, either solid or veneered. It apparently stands well the daily use and wear in our homes; and if, at any time, a piece becomes a trifle dull, a coat of brown wax or furniture polish quickly restores its sheen.

Table tops finished in this way are said not to withstand well the effect of damp glasses which have been used for serving the beverages prohibited by our zealous government at Washington. However, I have had no real experience with this reported objection, and, assuming that my readers are strict observers of the law, I might well have omitted reference to it.

OIL FINISH

In passing, I shall mention two other simple finishes which are satisfactory only on furniture made of hard, close-grained woods, such as maple, beech, birch, cherry, and mahogany. They should not be attempted on soft woods, such as pine and tulipwood.

Let us say, for example, that we have a maple lowboy which has been cleaned and carefully smoothed with fine sandpaper and steel wool. We may, if so inclined, try an oil finish, which consists simply of applying thin coats of boiled linseed oil, and thoroughly rubbing in each coat with a soft woolen cloth. No surplus oil should be left on the piece at any time, and, after the application of each coat of oil and the subsequent rubbing, the piece should be left in a warm room for twenty-four hours. The success of this oil finish depends on much friction, little oil, and certainly that no surplus oil is left on the piece to become gummy and sticky.

This oil finish is fairly satisfactory on hard, well-filled woods and very satisfactory on the tops of dining tables, but is a rather slow process, and I prefer the general-purpose finish, since it is in every way more satisfactory.

BUTCHER'S WAX FINISH

We might try on a similar maple lowboy the butcher's wax finish.

There are innumerable formulæ for butcher's wax. Beeswax in combination with various oils has been used for wood finishing since very ancient times. A satisfactory wax is made by melting one-half pound of yellow beeswax, and, while it is warm, adding one-half pint of turpentine, one-half pint of boiled linseed oil, and a small quantity of burnt umber to give the mixture a brown tone. This melting and mixing should be done in a double boiler, as the ingredients, when hot, are inflammable. With the butcher's wax finish, as with the oil finish, it is a matter of little wax and much-friction.

First apply a thin coat of wax, followed by hard rubbing with a woolen cloth. An interval to dry in a warm room, then more wax, and more rubbing. No surplus wax should be left when the piece is put away to dry, as this surplus will become sticky. Three or four well-rubbed coats of butcher's wax will give a soft, dull finish much admired by many collectors. But, again, I prefer the general-purpose finish.

A VOICE FROM THE PAST

The *Universal Receipt Book* published in Philadelphia in 1829, after describing the preparation of a furniture wax by melting together two ounces of yellow beeswax with four ounces of turpentine, goes on to say:

Many cabinetmakers are contented with waxing common furniture such as tables, chests of drawers, etc. This covering by means of repeated friction soon acquires a polish and transparency which resemble those of varnish.

Waxing stands shocks but does not possess in the same degree as varnish the property of giving lustre to the bodies on which it is applied. The lustre it communicates is dull, but this is compensated by the facility with which any accident to the polish may be repaired.

This admirable publication, which described everything that anybody could possibly want to know in the year 1829, also goes into the details of the approved method of refinishing furniture in that same year. We quote again:

DURABLE POLISH FOR FURNITURE

Take your table to the cabinetmaker and make him plane off the wax or varnish. Then take some very fine sifted brick dust, mix a little sweet oil with it, just enough to make it stick together like flour. Rub this mixture on the wood with a fine pumice stone until it is perfectly smooth: then add some spirit of wine or strong old whiskey and continue rubbing until you have the required polish, which will be more beautiful and far more durable than varnish. Water may be thrown upon it without injury and when by age the polish becomes dull, you can in five minutes restore its beauty by rubbing it with a cloth dipped in boiled oil or by using the brick dust, as at first.

I have for some time intended to try out this method but at the present writing the process remains untested. I fear that it would be difficult to really approve of that section wherein we are told "make him plane off the wax or varnish," nor of the use of rare old spirituous liquors in the compounding of a furniture polish—no matter how excellent.

THE RIGHT COLOR OF WOODS

All maple furniture may be given a beautiful golden tone by the application of *one* well-rubbed coat of *boiled* linseed oil before receiving the thin shellac coat which is the first step in our general-purpose finish. Every trace of surplus oil should be wiped off, and the piece should be put aside for twenty-four hours before shellacking. Linseed oil should not be used on fine oak or porous woods, as such woods absorb so much oil that their color becomes too dark. *Many persons object seriously to the darkening effect of linseed oil on cherry and pine.*

The general tone of old maple which has been properly

cleaned, smoothed, and finished, is a brownish yellow. It seems to be usual, at the present time, to want maple furniture to appear almost white. If the old surface of maple with its patina is thoroughly scraped and planed off, and the piece is finished with white shellac, it may be made so to appear.

New maple is almost white; but old maple is yellow, or brownish yellow, and good taste would indicate that we do nothing to make it look white and new. These same remarks apply equally to pine and tulipwood, which are very light colored when new, and yellow or brownish yellow when old.

The proper color on old mahogany is a varying shade of warm reddish brown. We have often seen fine pieces of mahogany which, after cleaning, had been stained a ghastly pinkish red, which is very far from the color of old mahogany. Some of the Empire and Early Victorian mahogany was stained very dark and now appears almost black. Bright red or pink mahogany furniture is an abomination.

WRONG WAYS AND THE RIGHT ONE

Let us draw a comparison between the wrong and right methods of restoring a piece of early American furniture. We shall assume that the piece in question is a fine, heavy, maple tavern table with good turnings and with the drawer, top, and cleats original. The top is slightly stained and marred. The stretchers are badly worn, but in place. The feet are missing, and must be restored. The table is a bit shaky and needs gluing. It carries several coats of old paint. Let us see what might happen to this table in inexpert and unsympathetic hands; also, what should result from proper and careful treatment.

A FRIGHTFUL EXAMPLE
UNDER THE WORST TREATMENT WE CAN IMAGINE

All the old pins are carelessly removed, and, since they are bent or broken, are thrown away. The table is taken entirely apart, and all the flat surfaces, including the top, drawer front, and stretchers, are deeply planed and scraped. The table is now glued and assembled, and new and badly fitting pins are driven into the old pin holes. The feet are restored with clumsy knobs of pine, not at all in accord with the old turnings, and these knobs are nailed on with long brads driven slantwise into the bottom of the posts.

The joint in the two-board top is filled with putty. The new pins, wherever exposed, show like white dots.

The turned legs are now deeply scraped, and the turnings left rough and jagged. The whole table is given a complete rubbing with coarse sandpaper, used both with and across the grain, thus leaving marks and scratches. The new feet are daubed with thin walnut stain, and a heavy coat of gaudy orange shellac is applied to the entire piece. The shellac accentuates every error; the marks of sandpaper all show; the new pins are white; and the restored feet are walnut color.

The table may now be said to be finished; and it is, indeed, *finished*, in so far as arousing interest or enthusiasm from a discriminating lover of old furniture is concerned.

The above description may seem exaggerated. It is not. Such methods are in common use. Every step in the work is wrong, and, as might be expected, the piece is a complete botch—skinned, scraped, daubed, and ruined.

A SUMMARY OF THE CORRECT
WITH CARE AND PROPER TREATMENT

The old pins are carefully removed and marked, so that they may be returned to their *same* holes and their same relative positions. An old pin exactly fits its original hole and no other.

The table is taken apart and the tenons of stretchers and skirt are reglued in place, care being taken not to spill surplus glue on the inside of the table. The old pins are restored to exactly their original positions in frame and top.

The feet are restored with proper turnings of old maple, which are doweled to the legs with strong pins.

The whole table is cleaned with varnish remover, possibly leaving a bit of old paint in the turnings, about pins, or under the top.

The table is given a careful and thorough rubbing with a suitable sandpaper. The top and the flat surfaces of the frame, if badly stained, may need a touch of the scraper, but such scraping will not be deep enough to make the old wood look like new. The table is finally rubbed with steel wool until every surface is smooth and silky.

The restored feet are treated with linseed oil and burnt umber, or other colors, until they harmonize with the old surfaces. The table is given two or three coats of a mixture of thin shellac and alcohol, well brushed in and smoothly applied, each coat being allowed to dry thoroughly. After that follows the process of waxing and rubbing.

The result is a table which still appears old, but is clean and sound, and glows with a subdued and honest finish. Its old pins, being end-grain wood, show darker than the other surfaces. No marks of the sandpaper or scraper appear. Marks of age and use are apparent on the top and on the worn stretchers. We may be proud of a table so treated, and we may know that it will not arouse in the soul of the expert a desire to imbibe a capacious and lethal tankard of the wood alcohol which was used in the work.

Not many years hence there will be little opportunity for us to restore or refinish fine early American furniture. Pieces then will not so often come to us "in the rough" from a minor dealer or ancient attic. They will reach us only through the dispersal of collections large or small, and the individual pieces will require little or no work. But, as things are now, my plea is that, when a fine piece of early furniture comes to us from the rapidly dwindling *original* supply, we treat it gently and reverently, preserving all its evidences of age and use.

Chapter VIII

BRASSES AND HARDWARE

SOME attention has already been given, in Chapter III, to the subject of brasses and handles. Original brasses are most desirable on our furniture, if we are so fortunate as to be able to acquire pieces thus equipped. It is probable that nearly all those used on the furniture of the American Colonies before the Revolution were produced in England, where the manufacture of such goods had attained a considerable magnitude and a great degree of perfection. At any rate, we find record of a steady flow of furniture brasses from England to the Colonies prior to this time. Genuine old brasses, particularly the sorts used early in the eighteenth century, will nearly always be made of very light-colored brass, which, when freshly polished, shows none of the deep golden color exhibited by the modern brass that contains a large percentage of copper. The amalgam used in early furniture brasses was high in zinc or tin—both light-colored metals—and low in copper. Some tendency toward darker shades of metal may be noticed on the handles made late in the eighteenth century, but these shades are not very dark or "brassy." After 1750 some of the brasses were, by a variety of methods, gilded on their surfaces, closely simulating the deep rich color of fine gold. This gold finish unless of the finest sort was not durable, and, when found on old brasses, is usually worn through and tarnished.

In judging the age of any piece of American furniture by its original brasses, there are a few considerations which should always be borne in mind. Styles changed slowly in the old days, transportation was difficult, and many communities and individuals were somewhat isolated. It is probable that not a few makers of furniture and a few stores in remote sections had in stock certain types of brasses whose styles had ceased to be in demand in Boston, Salem, Providence, New York and Philadelphia—communities quick to demand the newest fashion. We usually assume that any piece which possesses its original bail handles fastened with cotter pins was constructed not later than 1730. However, it is my opinion that many pieces thus equipped as to handles were turned out in remote sections as late as 1750. And the styles of provincial furniture itself, as well as the mounts, often trailed those of the sea-board cities and towns.

I own a simple cherry desk which, when purchased, had some of its original brasses still in place. These brasses were of the bail handle type, with two round plates held in place by bolts and nuts. Judging by these brasses, this desk should have been made between 1760 and 1775. Such is not the case; for I found written in ink, on the under side of one of the drawers, this notation:

September, 19th day, 1801.
I bote this deske of Lewis Burton of Stratford, Connecticut, for 4:—15.—6——paid all down by me.
Isaac Booth.

Lewis Burton, who was a cabinet-maker of Stratford, Connecticut, had, for some unknown reason, applied to this "deske," brasses which had been rather out of fashion for twenty-five years. We all very naturally desire to date our furniture at the earliest period possible, but if we do so entirely on the evidence of its original brasses, we may sometimes be mistaken.

Much old furniture will be found to have suffered considerable mutilation through the loss of handles and subsequent replacements. Very old pieces may display several varieties of brasses of widely different periods. Sometimes drawer fronts will be riddled with the holes bored for various sorts of handles of different spreads. An old chest of drawers may finally be relegated to the tool-shed, in a state of almost complete ruin, its only pulls being pieces of discarded leather harness applied with nails. It is most interesting to note on some very old drawer fronts the marks of the application of various types of handles. I have seen such drawers, which showed plainly that the original brasses had been of the single drop variety of 1700, applied with a single cotter pin, and the drawer fronts subsequently worn in a semi-circle by the swinging handle. These drop handles may have disappeared by 1730, at which time someone then bored two new holes and installed plates and bail handles held by two cotter pins. These may in turn have gone the way of most brasses by 1790, when new and larger holes were drilled to receive the bolts of the bail handles and the typical stamped oval plates of that late period. When these oval plate handles became broken, about 1840, the wide turned wooden knobs of the Victorian age were perhaps substituted in their place, or, maybe, after such a long career, the piece was counted of little worth, deserving only the application of cast-iron drawer knobs. At any rate, these many changes will often have left clear traces of just what was done; and while we dislike the marks of such changes with their mutilations, we certainly can hardly doubt the authenticity of a piece which shows them.

Plates 21-24 show typical specimens of furniture with their approximate dates below them. Beside each specimen of furniture has been drawn the appropriate style of handle and escutcheon for use in conjunction with it or with pieces of similar period and character.

Plates 25-27 show typical forms of brasses photographed from genuine and original examples, with some comment not only on the brasses but on their appropriate use. All or nearly all of these brasses illustrated, as well as innumerable other patterns, are to be had nowadays in excellent repro-

PLATE 21

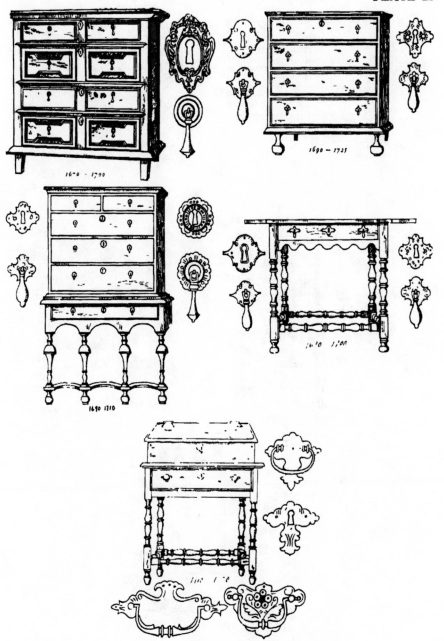

1670 - 1700

1690 - 1725

1690 1710

1670 1700

1700 1720

VERY EARLY AMERICAN FURNITURE WITH APPROPRIATE BRASSES

PLATE 22

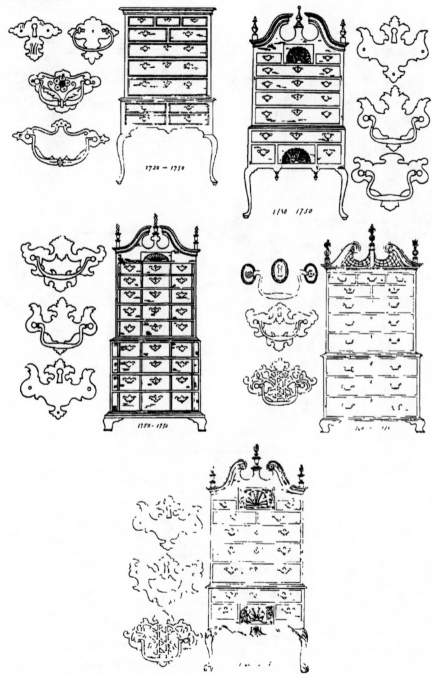

1720 — 1750

1730   1750

1750 — 1770

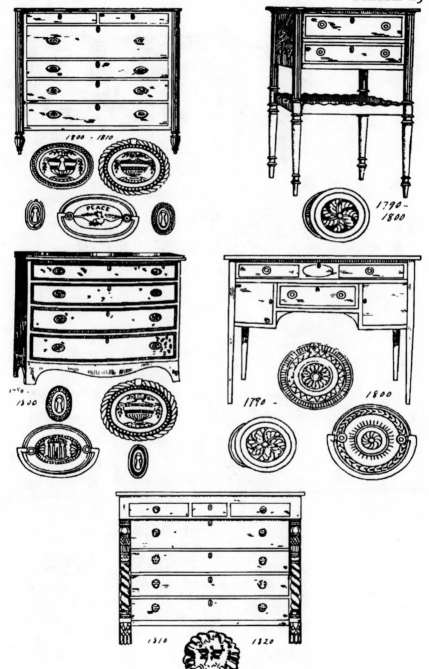

PLATE 23

1800 - 1810

PEACE

1790 - 1800

1790 - 1800

1790 - 1800

1810 - 1820

PLATE 24

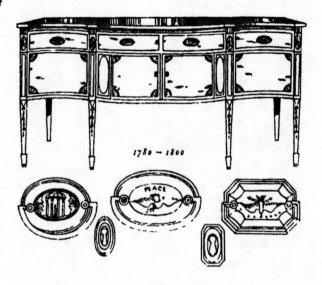

1780 – 1800

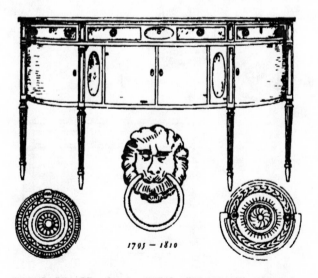

1795 – 1810

SIDEBOARDS OF 1780-1810 WITH APPROPRIATE BRASSES

PLATE 25

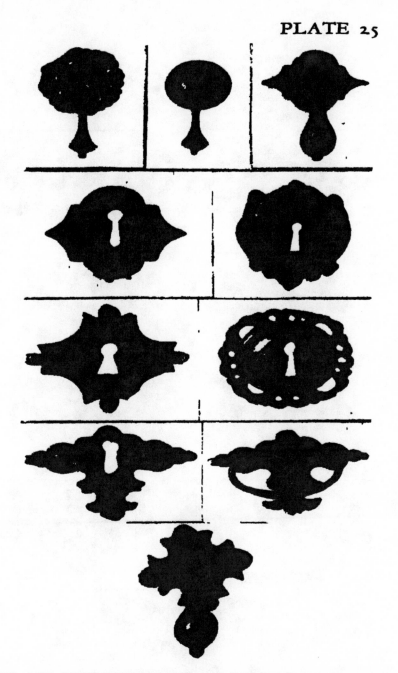

DROP- AND COTTER-PIN-BRASSES AND KEYHOLE ESCUTCHEONS
OF THE PERIOD 1690 TO 1730

PLATE 26

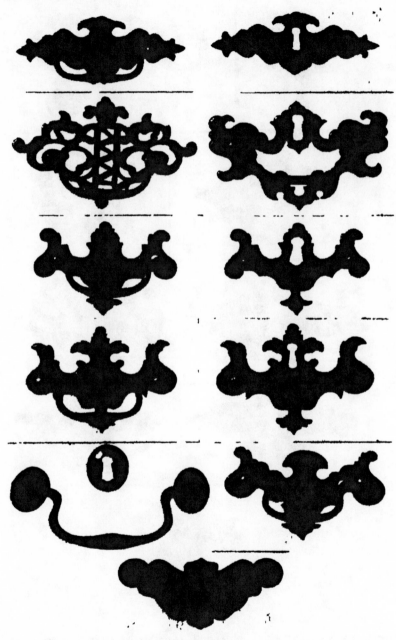

BRASSES AND ESCUTCHEONS—PERIOD 1730 TO 1780

PLATE 27

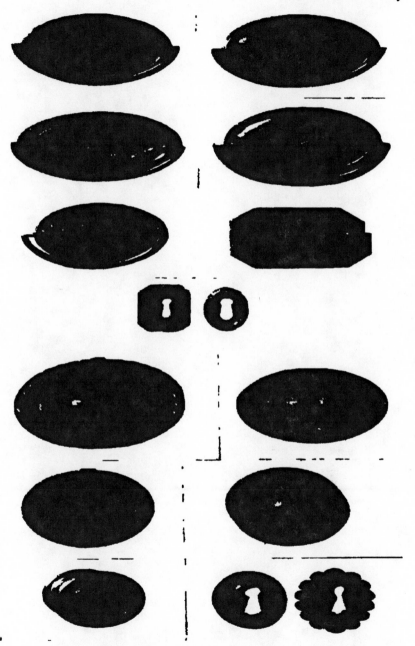

BRASSES AND ESCUTCHEONS 1780 1820

ductions. But, in purchasing reproduction brasses, certain considerations should be borne in mind:

First, the simpler the piece, the plainer should be its accompanying brasses.

Again, the charm of early brasses lies in their reasonable proportioning to the scale of the furniture. Simple pieces of pine furniture were not often equipped with large and ornate brasses, nor were fine and important pieces, such as highboys with broken-arch tops, often fitted with small, plain, and insignificant brasses.

We should, in so far as possible, utilize the holes drilled in our furniture for the original brasses. Reproduction brasses are made in many different sizes, and, if we first measure the distance of the old holes from centre to centre, we shall probably be able to obtain reproductions which will exactly fit them.

Very many pieces of our earliest American furniture— our court cupboards, chests, and chests of drawers—left their makers' hands quite unadorned with any metal handles or escutcheons. Quite commonly, drawers and doors were equipped with small turned wooden knobs as a means of opening. However, on many pieces thus finished with wooden knobs either plain or ornamental, iron or brass escutcheons were placed over keyholes, or the locations where keyholes would have been had the piece possessed locks. The use of small turned knobs on fine and important pieces of furniture was discontinued at an early date, although their use on tables and the small and more simple pieces persisted well on into the eighteenth century. To generalize broadly, we might say that the drawers of nearly all fine and important pieces of American furniture were, *after the year 1690*, equipped with brass handles and often with keyhole escutcheons.

The two chests of drawers shown at top of Plate 21 might, very properly, have been equipped with turned knobs of wood. Such knobs would have been most inappropriate on the six-legged highboy shown below them. Pieces of furniture with trumpet-turned legs, of the period from 1690 to 1720, ordinarily call for cast drop brasses. Handles and keyhole escutcheons do not always match, the latter being sometimes the more elaborate as in the 1 and 3, Plate 21. Some such pieces are found on which the original brasses were of the bail-handle type fastened upon the plate with two cotter pins. Trumpet-turned pieces equipped with bail handles are usually placed, as to date, toward the end of the trumpet-turned period (*c. 1720*).

When the period of symmetrical vase-shaped turnings is reached (*c. 1700*) drop handles should be sparingly used. Preference should usually be given to the bail handle of light construction, with a light back plate, plain or ornamented, but *not* pierced. In Plate 21, 4 bail handles would really be fully as appropriate as the drops, except for the small size of the table. Keyhole escutcheons were secured by tiny brass or iron nails.

The genuine old brasses shown in Plate 25 are all *cast* of light-colored brass. Such brasses are solid and are flat on the back. The first, second, fifth, and seventh examples have the ornamentation integrally cast in raised designs. The remaining examples were cast with flat surfaces and have the subsequent ornamentation which is usually called "engraving." However, this incised ornamentation is *not* the work of the graving tool but was done with small metal punches on the ends of which the desired pattern was raised. These punches were of a variety of simple designs: circles, semicircles, squares, diamonds, rows of dots, and bars of dots. They were impressed upon the flat surface of the plate by striking the upper end of the punch with a hammer. Makers of brasses could, with an assortment of punches, form different combinations of designs to suit their fancy. As the completed ornamentation of each brass plate was made with

PLATE 28

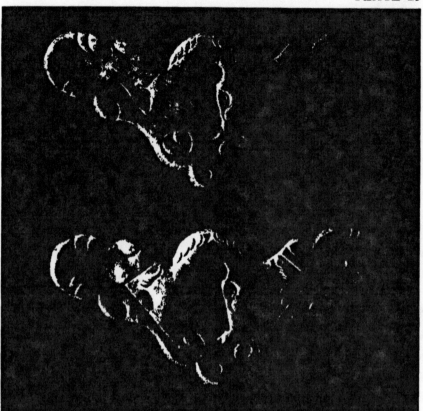

A   KEYHOLE ESCUTCHEONS FROM A SET OF COTTER-PIN BRASSES OF ABOUT 1725
Usually and erroneously known as "engraved," these brasses were cast and ornamented by means of hand-punches

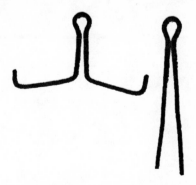

B   COTTER-PIN FASTENINGS OF EARLY BRASSES
The first is bent ready for clinching into the interior surface of

from ten to fifty separate impressions from these punches, and the work was done entirely "by eye," no two of these brasses were ever identical in pattern (Plate 28 A).

These early cast brasses often show file marks where the uneven edges of the castings were removed. All of the handles of the type shown in Plate 25 were held in place by cotter pins of round or flattened brass or iron wire, which, after being thrust through a small hole drilled in the drawer front, were clinched into the wood. We shall note on any piece of furniture having original cotter-pin brasses, that such brasses are usually fastened with *iron* cotter pins. Brass cotter pins were weak, and did not stand the strains of long use so well as those of iron. It would be extremely difficult ever to find a complete and original set of handles secured by original *brass* cotter pins. (Plate 28 B.)

When the eighteenth century was well under way, the drop handle no more appeared. Fastened with a single cotter pin and poorly designed to resist the strains of use, it was an unsound device. It was supplanted by the bail handle, fastened through the plate with *two* cotter pins—a much more dependable arrangement. Furniture began to take on elaborate forms, in which the cabriole leg and curves played an important part. On the earliest eighteenth century types, such as the highboy of Plate 22, 1, the engraved back plate with light bail handle fastened with cotter pins is appropriate. But such handles become heavier as the century progresses; the long tail of the back plate shrinks, and the fundamental form common to Chippendale furniture becomes dominant.

Of the brasses grouped in Plate 26 any of the forms shown in the second, third, and fourth rows of the centre group might be used, not improperly, on any one of the pieces of furniture shown in Plate 22, except that of No. 1. In this general connection, however, may be repeated the observation already made: *use simple brasses for simple pieces*. On great numbers of straightforward Pennsylvania walnut chests of drawers, chests, and highboys of the mid-eighteenth century, and on plain mahogany, maple, or cherry specimens from New England, the simple bail handle and round or oval bolt escutcheons with grooved or beaded edges can be used. Plates 26-29. It is always safe.

Brasses of the eighteenth century are relatively larger in scale than those of the previous century. Block-front pieces often carry very large pierced-pattern handles.

English furniture, and some pieces of American origin, of the mid-eighteenth century, occasionally carry brasses quite in the French fashion and highly elaborate. Since consideration of such exceptional types would here probably prove more confusing than helpful, it has not been attempted.

All of the bail handles of the original brasses shown in Plates 26 and 27 were held in place by *threaded brass bolts*, fastened by nuts either round, square, or hexagonal— sometimes merely irregular bits of sheet brass. The bolts were usually rather small in diameter and the threads coarse and rapid. See Plate 29. The bolts, as well as the bail handles, of old brasses will nearly always, except on massive pieces, give us an impression of being too light in weight to adequately serve their purpose. Had these metal parts been considerably heavier, we should now possess many more pieces of furniture, with complete sets of original brasses. However, were pieces thus equipped more common, we could not now so greatly enjoy boasting over their possession.

Almost all of these original early brasses will show, in sets, minor variations in shape. Some of them were cast, others cut by hand from sheet metal: none of them were the productions of cutting dies, and there is no exact uniformity of shape. The edges of these brasses were nearly always beveled and these edges often show the marks of the file. We shall note, in these later eighteenth century brasses, the declining use of any engraved or incised decorations: the surfaces were mostly flat and smooth, and decorative desire was appeased by increased size, a more elaborate outline, and perforation of the metal.

The variety of patterns of brasses, from which choice may be made, greatly increases when we come to deal with furniture of the period 1780–1830. The fundamental forms, however, during this late period, remain very nearly constant either as circles or as ellipses. Occasionally, too, we encounter rectangles whose corners have been clipped. In this period, brasses were no longer cast and engraved, or ornamented with a pierced pattern; they were made of thin metal *stamped in relief*, and their ornamental designs were entirely the work of dies. There was no variation in size, as in the older handmade brasses. These finely executed products of the diemaker's skill were produced in innumerable artistic patterns exhibiting hunter and dogs, grape and vine acorns and oak leaves, beehives, pheasants, eagles, crocodiles, serpents, lions, deer, the dove of peace, Roman temples and barges. This period produced the finest furniture brasses of all time, and mahogany, then so much in vogue, contributed the ideal background for the display of their gleaming and beautifully designed surfaces (Plate 27).

Some of the fine and delicate furniture handles of this type may be of silver or silver plate. We occasionally find the bail or ring handle giving way to the flat circular knob, particularly on smaller pieces. The face of this knob is sometimes decorated with a small rosette, sometimes with concentric circles. Ivory knobs occur on dainty sewing-tables, and keyholes are framed in ivory or light-colored wood.

It is virtually impossible to lay down rules as to choice of patterns among the innumerable designs which the stamping die has made available. In general, however, the circular or nearly circular back plates bearing a heavy urn design, of Roman or Pompeian suggestion, should be avoided in connection with the lighter-scale specimens of American furniture. They are really more appropriate on pieces of rather dark, rich mahogany, in which the classic influence of the Brothers Adam is more or less apparent. Such pieces are more frequently encountered among English than among American examples. Ring handles with a circular rosette back plate, however, have a wide measure of suitability.

In the case of old furniture of the late eighteenth century the shape of the handles required is usually determined by the hole marks of original applications. Sometimes the original holes have been plugged and a knob set between them. Examination of the inner side of the drawer-front will usually reveal the nature and style of the early handles.

In the case of sideboards, it will frequently be found that cupboard doors and bottle drawers show no indication of ever having been equipped with handles or knobs. Since drawers and cupboards of such pieces harbored articles whose preciousness required protection with a lock, a key frequently served all the requirements of a knob or handle. Where original knobs or the marks of them do not occur on sideboards, it may be the part of wisdom not to supply the deficiency. Victorian knobs or handles will sometimes be found as disfiguring late additions on the doors and deep drawers of old sideboards. In such cases, it is not always easy to decide whether completely to remove the excrescences and heal the resultant scars as well as may be, or to supply the most nearly correct substitute obtainable.

Toward the close of the eighteenth century and during the early years of the nineteenth, as furniture grew heavier, the apparent weight of hardware increased proportionately. The lion head carrying a ring handle belongs in the transition period between Sheraton and Empire, and serves as effectively on pieces that are classifiable as Empire as on those which must properly be known as Sheraton. On Empire pieces, such as the chest of drawers (Plate 23, 5), a large

PLATE 29

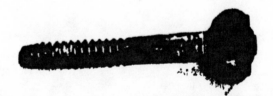

POSTS AND NUTS OF BRASSES
1, Good English Reproduction 2, 3, and 4, Old Posts and Shaped Nuts

form of knob was often used. In this period we may occasionally come across examples of simple plain pine or tulipwood furniture originally equipped with almost any of the later brasses. They are inconsistent but interesting examples of a combination of simplicity with extreme ornamentation.

GLASS FURNITURE KNOBS

While glass knobs may not be properly classed as brasses or hardware, we may well devote a few lines to objects which so intrigued the interest of the 1820's and 1830's.

These knobs were made largely of pressed glass in a wide range of patterns and in colors grave and gay—clear white, opaque white, opalescent white, true opal, deep and light blue, yellow, amber, black. Some were of mercury blown glass, and some were cut. They were equipped with brass bolts set into an orifice at the back of the knob by means of plaster of Paris. Often the brass bolts and nuts were plated in imitation of silver; and some glass knobs may be found on which the metal parts were of pewter. Quantities of these colorful knobs were turned out at Sandwich, Pittsburgh, and many of the other numerous American glass factories operating at that time. These glass knobs were fragile, and complete and intact sets which have come down to us from the comparatively recent time of their vogue are therefore not often encountered.

Many of these knobs have been reproduced; but, such was the diversity of size, design, and color in the originals, that if we need one or two to complete an old set, we shall very likely be unable to match them.

While glass furniture knobs call forth no cheers from that class of collector which seeks butterfly tables and chests of drawers with original cotter-pin brasses, we may acknowledge that the presence of these knobs upon a piece of late mahogany furniture does present a rather pleasing appearance—and they certainly portray a period in the history of our furniture handles which we may not completely ignore.

NAILS, TACKS, AND WOOD SCREWS

Hand-forged nails were used in some locations on our American furniture of the very earliest times. Simple six-board chests were constructed which were entirely held together by these nails, which, further, were commonly employed on drawers, moldings, cornices, and the backs of cabinet pieces. From an unknown source has come a mistaken but oft-quoted opinion that "nails are not old" and that "all antiques are put together with wooden pins." Some inexperienced collectors seem to look with suspicion upon any nails wherever they may be placed on early furniture. Nails are most certainly ancient devices and the hand-forging of nails was a most important industry in the American Colonies.

Of course the first hand-wrought nails were imported, and we know that, for a long time, nails and nail rods, largely made in England from fine Russian and Swedish iron, were brought into the Colonies. However, iron was produced in the Colonies by the middle of the seventeenth century; and probably this soft iron was beaten by hand into sheets and later formed into nails.

But in early times rolling and slitting mills were established and then turned out nail rods in various weights from native or Russian bar iron imported through England. The use, in hand-wrought nails, of a considerable quantity of this fine European iron probably accounts for their superior qualities. These nail rods were cut and forged by hand into the required sorts and sizes, and whole communities and families busied themselves with the making of nails, brads, and tacks. They must have worked hard, for the expression "to work like a nailer" is in country districts

PLATE 30

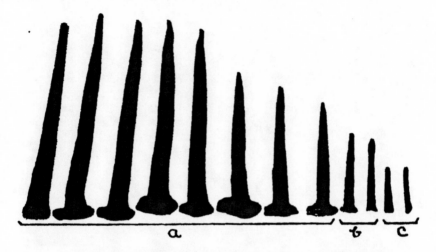

A   HAND-FORGED IRON NAILS AND BRADS WITH FLATTENED HEADS
a Nails   b Brads   c Tiny brads for mouldings and escutcheons

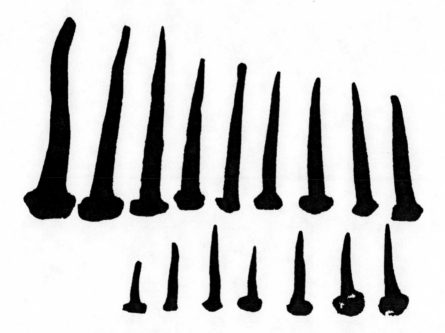

B   HAND-FORGED NAILS AND BRADS WITH ROUNDED HEADS

still used to denote a condition of intense and feverish industry.

Hand-forged nails were made from soft, fine iron of a very good quality. They were strong and tough: they bent easily but did not break. The density of texture produced by intense heat and hand-forging made them extremely resistant to rust and dampness. They were the honest productions of an honest age. Where modern cut-iron nails disintegrate in twenty-five years of exposure, some of these hand-forged nails are intact after a century and a half of similar conditions. From the oak timbers of old houses, I have often pulled nails which still had upon them the blue scale which all hand-forged iron possesses. As no two handmade articles are ever exactly alike, so each hand-forged nail is slightly different from any other. They were made in a wide variety, from the large spikes used in ship-building to the tiny brads for fastening the escutcheons on furniture. They were made with a number of different kinds of head, and either sharp or flattened points—depending on their intended purpose. Dozens of names identified the different sorts: rose, clasp, deck, clout, counter-clout, clench, cooper, dog, and horseshoe. The two sorts of large hand-forged nails which were most commonly used on our furniture were both made with long, sharp points, and square shanks. One variety had a round head, showing irregular marks of the hammer; the other a flattened or folded head. The smaller hand-forged nails, or brads, used for fastening moldings and brasses often had a very small head, while the small nails used for the application of H, HL, and butterfly hinges had large circular heads. The points, when the nails were thus used were clinched and turned back into the wood. All of these hand-forged nails were of tough metal, bent easily, and did not break when clinched. (Plate 30).

Hand-forged tacks had every appearance of tiny hand-forged nails. They were, of course, made in a variety of sizes, with both large and small heads, on which marks of the hammer often appeared. Their points were very sharp, and the iron used in their making was of fine quality.

Toward the end of the eighteenth century and early in the nineteenth, our native inventive genius devoted much attention to the production of nails by machinery, and dozens of patents, mostly by New England inventors, were recorded for machines to produce cut-iron nails. The first patent was granted to Ezekiel Reed of Bridgewater, Massachusetts, in 1786, for a "cut-nail machine"; and within twenty years the old hand-forging methods had been pretty thoroughly displaced by the automatic machines. The new cut nails, or, as they were sometimes then called, "cold nails," were made of the same fine iron that had been used in the hand-forged nails and they were strong and durable, although they lacked the toughness and consolidation of material which come with intense heat and hand-forging.

The cut-nail machines worked rapidly, and their product could be sold at one-third of the price of the hand-forged nails; hence, as has often occurred, a very superior but costly handmade device was displaced by the less worthy but cheaper product of a machine.

Cut-iron nails, like hand-forged nails, were made in many varieties, large and small, but the major part of the larger sizes were made square on the point. These nails were driven with the widest part of the shank set parallel with the grain of the wood, so that the square end punched out a cross-section of the fibre, and splitting was thus obviated. Cut-iron nails were somewhat used until within the last generation, but at the present time wire nails have apparently quite supplanted them.

When we attempt to date furniture by the type of nails employed in its construction, we cannot reasonably date any piece made with machine-made cut nails very much back of 1790. However, if a piece is constructed with real hand-

PLATE 31

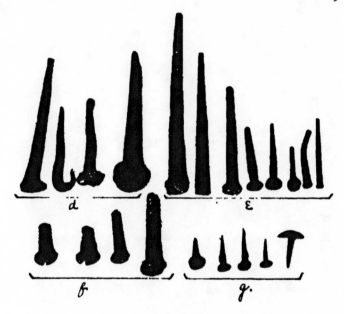

A   NAILS, SCREWS, AND TACKS

d Unusual styles   e Cut-iron machine-made nails   f Hand-made square-end wood screws   g Hand-wrought tacks and cast-brass upholstery tack

B   HINGES USED ON EARLY FURNITURE

forged nails, we have every reason to hope that it was made previous to 1790. Here, again, we must remember that, very probably, in some isolated sections hand-forged nails were produced in a diminishing quantity long after cut nails had come into general use; also that some individuals may have had on hand considerable stocks of hand-forged nails. In ancient attics within the last few years, I have come across several lots of these old nails—unused, straight, and as clean as if newly from the forge.

The change from hand-forged to cut-iron tacks, with the attendant automatic machine methods of manufacture, closely paralleled the transition from hand-forged to cut-iron nails.

The iron tacks which we use today to hold our carpets in place are virtually identical in appearance with the iron tacks produced by the automatic tack machines of 1810.

I cannot recall ever having seen anywhere, in any piece of our typical seventeenth century furniture, a single wood screw which seemed to have been originally used in its construction. I have seen such pieces repaired with wood screws, but such repairs were probably made long after the piece was constructed. While hand-forged nails were much employed in seventeenth century furniture, if wood screws were at all used, such use would seem to have been extremely uncommon.

When we advance into the eighteenth century, we begin to find a considerable use of wood screws, particularly in fastening table hinges. Most of the drop-leaf tables made close to the year 1700 possessed tongue-and-groove joints and the hinges were applied with small nails, often clinched or riveted on the upper side of the leaves. When the rule joint came into general use upon drop-leaf tables, about 1725, we shall probably find that the hinges were applied with wood screws, which accomplished their purpose without completely penetrating the wood and marring the appearance of the table top. All of the screws of that time were, very evidently, handmade: they were rough, the threads were coarse, and the slots at the top were of uneven depth, and frequently cut off-centre. These screws did not have the gimlet point of the modern machinemade wood screw, but were cut squarely off on the lower end; and it is very evident that a hole must have been drilled for the reception of every screw since the square ends would quite prevent the penetrative ability of the modern wood screws. The production of these square-end wood screws entirely by means of hand labor was probably a slow operation, and such screws are said to have been very expensive.

A slowly increasing use of wood screws may be observed on our furniture after 1750. Screws were then often used in locations where nails or wooden pins had formerly been employed. Table tops, which previously had been fastened to their frames with wooden pins, were then secured by long screws run slantwise through the inner side of the frame and thus into the under side of the top. The cross cleats placed under the tops of candlestands and oval-top tables began to be fastened with screws instead of hand-forged nails, and a similar change was made in the means of fastening the triangular forged-iron contraption which was placed beneath the bottom of the pedestal turning of tripod tables and stands to prevent the legs from spreading. Nevertheless, these were all locations hidden from view when the furniture was in use. We sometimes find screws fastening H, HL, or any ornamental hinges exposed on the surfaces of cupboards, and particularly brass hinges.

Early in the nineteenth century, many patents were recorded for screw-cutting machines, and by 1820 great quantities of wood screws were being rapidly turned out by machines which were entirely automatic.

When we examine the screws used on furniture of this period, we shall find a decided improvement in their appearance. They are no longer rough and irregular as were the earlier handmade screws, but show in many ways that they are the result of positive machine methods. However, they still continued to be made with square ends, and it was not until the middle of the nineteenth century that the gimlet-point wood screw appeared. Many patents were recorded and much litigation resulted, but by 1860 the American Screw Company had, by purchase of patents and the possession of automatic machinery, a virtual monopoly of the manufacture of gimlet-point wood screws in the United States. The decided advantage of this sort of screw rendered the older square-end screw quite unsaleable and it soon became obsolete.

And so we cannot accurately date our furniture by the wood screws used in its construction; but we are pleased when we find that the hinges of some drop-leaf table, which we hope was made about 1750, are fastened with rough and poorly made square-end screws. And we should not let the presence of some gimlet-point screws, in usual or unusual locations, influence us strongly against any piece, as such screws have been much employed, during the last seventy-five years, in repairing our old furniture.

ORNAMENTAL HINGES

I am not at all sure that the hand-forged hinges which were placed upon the outer surfaces of our early furniture may properly be called "ornamental," but to distinguish them from the plain hinges used on drop-leaf tables, desk lids, and cupboard doors—locations where they were hidden from sight—let us use this term. H, HL, or butterfly hinges certainly appear to us as ornamental features when found upon the doors of cupboards, and they are always to be preferred to the hidden butt hinge.

Of these "ornamental hinges" used on our early furniture, there is no great variety to illustrate or describe.

The butterfly is our earliest style of hinge. It was made in a variety of sizes and the iron of the spread ends was usually much thinner than the central section. Butterfly hinges were used in many locations on our early furniture, and, not only in exposed positions, but on the tongue-and-groove points of our earliest drop-leaf tables. They were fastened with hand-wrought nails clinched or riveted. Original butterfly hinges on any piece of early American furniture are considered an evidence of great age, and, while dates are dangerous, we might feel reasonably sure that a piece thus equipped was made prior to the year 1750. We shall note in our travels that furniture possessing original butterfly hinges is not often encountered.

Fig. 16. Butterfly Hinge

H and HL hinges were extensively used throughout the eighteenth and, to some extent, in the first quarter of the nineteenth century chiefly on the doors of cupboards of various sorts. They were hand-forged and usually show marks of the hammer. The ends were sometimes cut into ornamental *fleur-de-lis* or circles, as in our illustration. Apparently the iron hinges were nearly always originally applied with nails, but toward the end of their time, cut nails and screws were sometimes employed.

Fig. 17. H Hinges

THE RAT-TAIL HINGE

The rat-tail hinge was commonly used on Pennsylvania and New York cupboards throughout the eighteenth century. It seems not to have been at all used in New England, unless in western Connecticut. The rat-tail hinge was sometimes applied with hand-forged nails, but often with rivets headed over iron washers at the back of the door. One advantage of the rat-tail hinge was that the doors could be removed by simply lifting them from the pins.

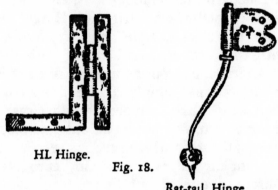

HL Hinge.

Fig. 18.

Rat-tail Hinge

Strap hinges were used to some extent on doors of cupboards, but never enjoyed the popularity of the H and HL varieties in this position. Innumerable variations of the strap hinge were used to fasten the lifting tops of chests. Their

Fig. 19.   Strap Hinges

longer ends were usually formed into round or spear-point designs.

All of these hinges were hand-forged, and were usually thinned down toward their edges and ends. They may show on their surfaces broad marks of the hammer, but these hammer-marks are incidental to the process of hand-forging, and not intentional or made with any idea of ornamentation. Many of the modern iron reproductions, especially those produced by factory methods, are frightful. Hinges described in catalogues as "real colonial style" will, very likely, be coarse, clumsy, with thick edges, and battered with the hammer until their surfaces are a continuous area of mars and dents; or the flat surfaces may simply receive a few coy and scattered wallops with a ball hammer; in either case the result is like nothing ever turned out by an old-time blacksmith.

There are small forges which produce very fair ironwork; but, when I want any hinges or ironwork reproduced I take a genuine sample to one of our Connecticut country blacksmiths, and he will give me exactly what I want. Most of these men are clever and ingenious, and their work is turned out by exactly the same methods used one hundred or two hundred years ago. Thus we obtain ironwork which is simple and right, and with no silly "artistic" or modern touches.

DROP-LEAF TABLE HINGES

The hinge used at the joints of our earliest drop-leaf tables was the butterfly. Gate-leg and butterfly tables old enough to be constructed with the tongue-and-groove joint were often equipped with the butterfly hinge, fastened with nails. Screws seem never to have been used for such fastening.

Succeeding to and overlapping the period of the butterfly came the hand-forged rectangular table hinge. This hinge was frequently, but not always, made—as was the butterfly—by cutting thin sheet-metal into a doubled pattern of each end-section. The doubled pattern was then folded upon itself over a pin and firmly welded, forming one end-member of the hinge. That this method was much used is very apparent when we examine old broken and rusty hinges, for the two layers of iron have often become separated, or we can see, on the side edges of the hinge, the line of the weld. The welding and hammering frequently caused the ends of this hinge to thin out and spread a bit, not like the ends of the butterfly, but enough so that the hinge did not remain exactly rectangular. This sort of table hinge was nearly always fastened in place with square-end wood screws, and the metal was sometimes reamed out for the reception of their heads. This hinge seems usually to accompany the rule joint on the drop-leaf tables made after 1725. We should hardly expect to find it on many tables made before this time, but, as has been remarked, "when we date we guess."

The rectangular table hinge was used throughout the last three-quarters of the eighteenth century and the entire nineteenth century. As time went on, this hinge showed a progressive refinement similar to that of the wood screw, and such hinges on a piece of furniture made late in the eighteenth century are likely to be exactly rectangular and to exhibit fewer marks of handwork. After the first quarter of the nineteenth century, these hinges quite supplanted H and HL hinges on cupboard doors, with a corresponding loss in the attractiveness and interest of these pieces.

Early in the nineteenth century, heavy cast-iron rectangular hinges came into vogue. They were thick, clumsy, heavy, and brittle, but we often find them on the furniture of that time. I have never seen them originally used upon any furniture which could be placed within the confines of the eighteenth century.

The staple hinge, also sometimes known as the clinch or cotter-pin hinge, was used in many locations on our early furniture. It was very commonly placed on the lids of six-board chests, sometimes on the lids of desks, and on cupboard doors. It seems to have been little used on drop-leaf table joints.

This hinge was constructed merely of two iron cotter pins hooked together, their ends being forged into long sharp points. The pins were thrust into holes bored slantwise through the opposing edges of the boards and the sharp ends clinched back into the wood. This hinge was a sound me-chanical device; it could be produced quickly by any blacksmith, and it enjoyed a wide use.

However, for some reason its employment seems to have declined through the last half of the eighteenth century and, by the end of the century it was quite obsolete. We should hardly expect that any piece of furniture equipped with staple hinges could be dated as of the nineteenth century.

CASTERS

There seems to be a widespread but erroneous feeling that casters are a comparatively modern device, and that no piece of early furniture ever originally possessed them. Casters equipped with leather rollers were used upon English furniture early in the eighteenth century. Later in the same century a great variety of casters was turned out, with plain cast and decorative brass sockets and brass or iron rollers. Some of the sockets were square; others were round, hexagonal, or octagonal. In Empire days many of the heavy pedestal tables were supported upon large and ornate cast-brass animal-paw feet, with casters set into the underside. Casters are most certainly old devices, and on heavy pieces of furniture their presence is often decidedly convenient.

We have many records of the early importation into the Colonies of casters along with brass furniture-fittings and hardware. A great many American tables and sofas, particularly those of the type known as Hepplewhite, Sheraton, and Duncan Phyfe, were originally fitted with casters. Casters which frankly show by their method of application that they have been added some time after the piece was finished are often found on chairs, desks, chests of drawers, lowboys, highboys, and all sorts of furniture. These later additions

PLATE 32

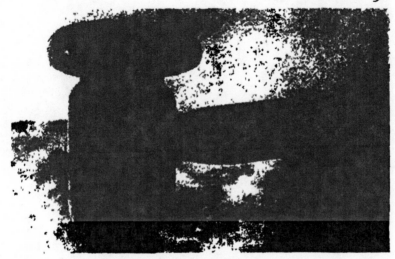

A THE MUSHROOM ARM OF A CHAIR 200 YEARS OLD

B. THE UNDER SIDE OF AN AUTHENTIC SMALL STAND
Note chamfered edge and hand-forged nails

cannot be dated and prove nothing as to the age of any example.

In general I may observe that it is seldom wise to attempt to determine the date of any piece of furniture on the basis of easily removed attachments, such as brasses, casters, superficial pieces of trim, and the like. Such elements are quite liable to have undergone changes and replacements during the life of the piece of furniture on which they appear. It is best, therefore, to judge the date, or period, of a piece of furniture on the basis of its style and structure, and thereafter to decide whether the hardware is correct and in keeping with the character of the piece.

Chapter IX

EVIDENCES OF AGE, USE, WEAR, AND AUTHENTICITY, WITH COMMENTS ON FRAUDS AND FRAUDULENT METHODS

IF WE are to collect early American furniture we may very well give careful thought to the matter of just how age, use, and wear have affected genuine examples. Each piece carries its own record, easily read and understood. Any piece of old furniture, either varnished, painted, or in the natural wood, which is quite intact and unrestored, exhibits a pleasing aspect of completeness and sincerity. The colors of all its surfaces are consistent and right, and the effects of wear and discoloration show in exactly the right places. Such a piece may be turned over, examined from every angle, scrutinized with the greatest care, and yet not a single detail will cause the slightest suspicion or doubt. A hundred experts may look it over, but not one will have any criticism: the piece is "right."

COLOR AND TEXTURE OF OLD SURFACES

A careful study of the color of the hidden and unfinished surfaces of old furniture is most interesting. The backs of chests of drawers and highboys were intended to be placed against a wall, and so were left in the natural wood. Age has darkened their surfaces to an even brown color; it may be a light brown or a very dark brown, but, in any case, an *even shade* of brown. The back of the upper section of a highboy has become the same shade of brown as the back of the lower section. All the boards forming the back of a chest of drawers will show the same uniform shade of brown.

If we examine the inside and unfinished surfaces of a

PLATE 33

THE WORN SIDE-STRETCHER OF AN AUTHENTIC BUTTERFLY TABLE
Note that the stretcher is almost intact under the lower end of the "ear"

highboy, we shall probably observe that the wood is a much lighter shade of brown than the outer surfaces of the back because the inner surfaces were not so greatly exposed to light and dust. However, on these inner surfaces we shall find the same evenness of color and texture. If a chest of drawers has four drawers, they shall all show the same shade of brown on their unfinished inner surfaces.

It is surprising how some woods—such as tulipwood and basswood—when used in locations where they were but little exposed to the light, as in drawers, will after a century or more still appear light in color and as new as if they had been made within the past decade. Therefore, if all other details of an old piece are right, while the basswood or tulipwood sides, backs, and bottoms of the drawers look very new, do not for this reason suspect the piece and pass it by. Pine, however, becomes darker with age—to a greater degree in exposed locations, but to a considerable degree in any location.

If an entirely original tavern table is turned upside down, the inner, unfinished surface of the frame and that portion of the top enclosed by the frame will show not only the same shade of brown, but the same texture and "bloom," and "feel." We can plainly see that the top is the original top and its enclosed under surface along with the inside of the frame has been aged by the same elements of time, dust, smoke, and moisture. The under side of the top *outside* the frame may be smeared with paint, or stained by grease, or marred by the marks of many scratched matches, but the surfaces inside the frame have by their location escaped these marks.

The backs of original looking-glasses often show a shade of brown which is almost black. When unfinished wood is thus slowly darkened by time, a strange, dark opacity of surface is produced, and any grain or figure in the wood is obscured. This appearance is difficult to describe; but when we are familiar with it, we can recognize it at once—and also easily recognize the efforts of the unscrupulous to treat new woods with stains and dyes so as to simulate age.

When any entirely original piece of genuine furniture is cleaned off with varnish remover, it still exhibits on all of its outer surfaces this same consistency of color. A maple chest of drawers which has been painted black shows, on "cleaning off," a shade of color on its surface different from that on a similar chest which has been painted red. But both will appear with an even and consistent coloring on their surfaces after the "cleaning off." The matter of color is one over which the furniture-faker usually stumbles. If he makes his reproductions of new woods, his efforts to age either the exposed or hidden surfaces with stains and dyes and acids are not at all plausible or convincing, if we are familiar with *genuine* old surfaces.

If the faker attempts to use old wood only he has great difficulty in finding a sufficient quantity of wood of even color; and if he tries artificially to bring all the various surfaces to the same color, he does not obtain uniformity, and again stumbles. We often hear, in these days, of marvelous, secret, overnight methods of changing new furniture into "genuine antiques." Some of these fraudulent products do sell to the gullible, but they do not confuse the expert.

Any collector who wishes to become familiar with the intricacies of color and texture of old surfaces—particularly hidden, inside, and unfinished surfaces—should avail himself of every opportunity to examine such surfaces on old furniture which he knows to be genuine.

LEGITIMATE WEAR ON FURNITURE

The evidences of wear and use on early furniture may be the subject for much thought, study, and conjecture. Wear may be great or small, depending on age and the conditions of use under which furniture has been placed. The evidences

PLATE 34

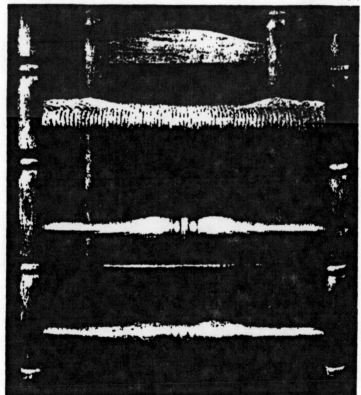

THE WORN RUNGS OF AN AUTHENTIC SLAT-BACK CHAIR
The upper rung receives much less wear than the lower This chair is original except for the removal of rockers
and the restoration of feet

of wear and use vary on different pieces of similar type, and occasionally we find a genuine piece which seems to have suffered almost no wear. It may have been a family heirloom, carefully treasured by many generations in the best room of an ancient home. Occasionally it may be so perfect as momentarily to arouse our suspicions. However, almost all early furniture is worn in various ways and if very old is often badly worn. Early furniture usually shows, on all exposed locations, a complete lack of knife-like edges or sharp corners. Wear and use have removed them. Old table tops, edges and corners of drawer fronts, the outer corner of all squared posts of tables and chairs, and the feet of all sorts of old furniture are nearly always rounded by use. We nowhere find any sharp edges except in places quite protected by their location. The inner corner of a squared chair post under the seat, or the inside edges of the square posts of a cabinet piece may be as sharp as when first constructed, for the reason that no wear came upon them.

The front edge of the feet of all small chairs is usually more rounded and worn than the back edge of the back feet. Whenever these chairs were moved, they were usually lifted by the backs and hung so that the front edges of the front legs struck the floor first and consequently became more rounded and worn. Sometimes chairs were tipped back against the wall by their lounging occupants and the back of the back legs became rounded, but the front legs are usually the more worn.

It is impossible by tipping a chair about on a level floor to bring any wear on the inside edges of the feet, and so these edges, if they have never suffered decay, will be much less rounded than are the outer edges. That part of the feet which comes into contact with the floor will often be found finely polished by wear and almost black in color. The patina or polish is sometimes scratched and marred, as shown in our illustration, Plate —, but if everything else is right this is an additional assurance of authenticity.

Countless feet left their effect upon the upper edges of the stretchers of tavern tables, but this wear was usually greater on the *outer* upper edge and in the *centre* of the stretcher, diminishing toward the posts. A much less amount of wear will show on the *lower outer edge*, and *hardly any* will appear on the *inner lower edge* of the stretchers. If the table contained a drawer, the stretchers on the *opposite* side from this drawer will usually show the least wear of any, as, during part of its long career, such a table would probably have been placed against a wall with the drawer facing outward.

The side stretcher of a genuine butterfly table is a beautiful example of legitimate wear. The lower end of the wing has protected the stretcher from all wear at its point of entry and so the stretcher is worn, on its outer upper edge, into two shallow waves with their crest directly under the lower end of the wing. (See Plate 33.)

When a tavern table is dishonestly converted into a butterfly table, the even wear on the long side stretcher of the tavern table is seldom considered by the faker, and when the fraudulent "butterfly" has come forth from its chrysalis, it shows a very tell-tale feature—the wear on the stretchers just under the lower end of the wing is as great as at any other point, thereby proclaiming that something is wrong with the lepidopterous insect.

The wear on chair rungs may be carefully considered. When a chair has two rungs at the front, the lower one is always the more worn. The side rungs will not be so badly affected as the front ones, but the *lower* side rungs will be more worn than the upper ones. (Plate 34).

The back section of the arm rail of a Windsor armchair is always more worn on the inside than the outside, as this rail never touched the wall or encountered much friction.

Children's turned chairs were usually and naturally abused

PLATE 35

THE WORN FINIAL OF A MAPLE SLAT-BACK CHAIR
Finials are usually most worn at the back where they come in contact
with the wall

by their small owners and frequently the front and back posts are worn flat from skidding over the floors.

Drawer runs will show a delightful and consistent wear. The upper drawers in the top section of a highboy were less easily reached than the lower ones, and consequently were more infrequently used: accordingly the drawers of a high-boy or chest will usually be found to be worn in exact ratio to their accessibility. On the other hand, the upper drawers of a four-drawer chest were opened without bending over, and so were given the preference in storing those articles which were most often required.

The finials of turned chairs nearly always show the re-sults of friction, but most of the wear is directly at the back, where they were rubbed against the walls. (Plate 35). The two outer sides of the finials will always be worn more than the inner sides, which could not, in any position, come into contact with the wall. On tall four- and five-slat-back chairs the wear on the posts is usually more pronounced where the shoulder blades and upper back of the occupant came into contact with them. In Plate 18, *B* it may be seen that, at exactly this point, the scoring marks are almost obliterated by long-continued wear, while the same marks at higher and lower points on the posts are still very clear.

I recently inspected a small open-top cupboard bearing on its single lower door an interesting example of legitimate wear. This door was intended to be held shut by a button-latch of wood, but had no knob with which to pull the door open. The various users had thus been forced to apply a finger or two on the edge of the door toward the top, result-ing in a long, slanting depression at this point—quite an inch in depth, and finely smoothed and polished. Such an example of wear should be left "as is" and no attempts made to restore it.

I once saw in Maine a simple pine chest with four drawers. The drawers were of the lipped type and had never been equipped with knobs or pulls, so the only way to open them was to use one's fingers under the lips at either end. This means of opening had evidently been followed for a very long time, as the front edges of the end boards were deeply worn at exactly the points where the users' finger-nails had come into contact with them. I wondered how many different women had remarked to how many different heedless men-folk, "I don't see why you don't get some knobs for this old chest," and they probably received the invariable reply, "I will, Ma, the next time I go to town"—but no one had ever made good the promise.

It is unnecessary to go further. My purpose has been to centre the attention of collectors on this most important subject. If we examine fine and original pieces of early furniture with the particular intent of studying the legitimate wear which they have endured, we open our minds to a fascinating field for surmise and deduction. Every original piece carries, plainly written over its various parts and surfaces, an accurate and absolutely authentic record of its age and treatment. It is worn where it should be worn, and quite unworn where no wear was encountered. When we train ourselves to observe all details of color and legitimate wear on early furniture, and put into practice some of the methods of deduction used by the very keen Mr. Sherlock Holmes, many of the frauds and fakes of the antique world will become childish in their ostrichlike inaccuracies.

OLD PAINTS

When we are considering the authenticity of pieces of furniture which are painted, a number of matters are to be considered. Very thick old paint is extremely hard and brittle, and will shatter under a hammer blow. Old paint, when experimentally scraped with a knife, comes away in tiny chips or powder, as the elasticity of the oil has been lost. New paint retains more or less of its elasticity for several

PLATE 36

A   THE UNDER SURFACE OF THE BALL FOOT
OF A CHEST OF ABOUT 1725

B   BIT HOLES

Left, Hole of Square-end gimlet point bit used since about 1850; Two Right, Round-end holes
of the ancient pod bit

years and when scraped is more likely to prove softer and less glasslike. When we scrape heavy paint very recently applied it will come off in strips and narrow ribbons.

A piece of early furniture may have on its surfaces anywhere from one to a dozen coats of paint of various colors applied at irregular intervals. A small section of every surface of such a piece will exhibit, if scraped to the wood, the same strata or layers of paint; and the scraped section will appear somewhat like our illustration, Fig. 20. Here A represents a small area of the wood scraped clean and we will imagine that B was a first coat of black paint, C a second coat of red, D a third coat of gray, and E a fourth coat of bright green. In such a case the edges of each layer will show plainly under a reading glass. On an original and intact piece of furniture every part should exhibit the same strata of paints in the same order. If this order on the under body of a Windsor armchair is black, red, gray, bright green, and black, the order of the paint layers will be the same on the back edge of the seat, the arm rail, and spindles. Therefore, if we

Fig. 20. Layers of Old Paint

should find upon scraping a small section, that the paint layers on the under body of a Windsor chair are black, green, blue, red, green, and black, while the layers on the rail are red, blue, red, green, and black, gray, and black, we would at once surmise that something was wrong. Only recently I "cleaned off" a Windsor chair which bore on all its surfaces eleven coats of paint, but they were arranged in the proper order on every part.

It is interesting to note how old, heavily painted Windsor chairs nearly always show splashes of the various colored paints on the underside of the seat where the four legs are inserted. These careless splashes of paint will sometimes give us a complete lapped color-card of the shades we may expect to find when the chair is cleaned off.

We should bear in mind that paint is one of the furniture-faker's best friends and is often used on partially genuine old furniture to cover new parts and restorations. However, such work usually consists of merely applying to the new parts a single coat of paint to conform in color with the old surfaces. Very seldom does the faker go to the trouble of covering the new parts with exactly the same successive color layers found on the original surfaces.

Amateur finishers are sometimes startled and surprised on applying solvents on a painted piece to see some brand new parts quickly emerge from under a single recent coat of paint. The solvents will uncover these replacements and repairs long before they will begin to have any dissolvent effect on the old and flintlike paints covering the original parts. When we have thought that a piece was entirely original, it is of course disappointing to come unexpectedly upon even minor replacements and new parts, thus camouflaged, but it does not at all mean that the piece is of little account. It may be a very good example which we must remove from the class of "all original" to that of having suffered "minor restorations."

If we are offered a piece of antique furniture all the surfaces of which have apparently been painted within a few years our suspicions are aroused, but this recent coat of paint does not actually prove that anything is wrong. Many fine pieces of early furniture have, in their home environments and within the past decade, received a fresh coat of paint. I once saw a fine old maple low-boy which had shortly before been enameled white to conform in color with the modern furniture of a bedroom In such a case the construction and the appearance of the inner surfaces would have the greater weight in influencing our judgment.

PLATE 37

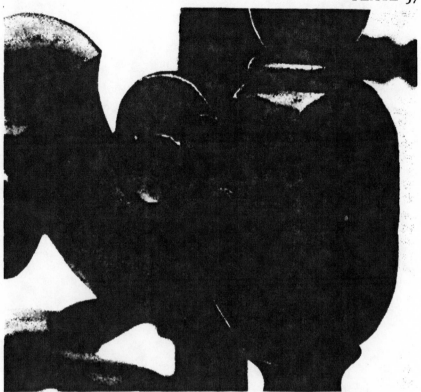

A. PROJECTING DIAMOND-SHAPED PIN IN AN AUTHENTIC AMERICAN CHAIR OF FLEMISH STYLE

B. SECTION OF TOP OF TAVERN TABLE WITH ONE OF THE ORIGINAL
PINS PROJECTING ABOVE SURFACE

Factory-made reproductions of new wood in the hands of the unscrupulous, and fraudulent furniture constructed of both old and new woods are often treated to several coats of paint of different colors and then partially cleaned with lye. Butterfly tables, being of a very valuable type, are often the objects of such intended deception. One weak point in any such work is that the new paints retain their elasticity and will not at all delude the wise collector.

OLD WOODEN PINS

As we have previously mentioned, the pins on early furniture are very seldom exactly round. They are oval, octagonal, square, and all sorts of shapes *except round*. The pins on reproductions are very often as round as if turned by a lathe. Old pins frequently project noticeably from the surrounding surfaces, while the round pins of reproductions are usually cut off exactly flush with the surfaces. (Plate 37, A).

The maple or oak pins used to hold in place pine or tulipwood table tops were, of course, very hard, and wore down more slowly than the softer boards into which they were driven. Thus we may find the large oak pins in the pine top of an original tavern table projecting one-eighth of an inch above the surface of the surrounding wood. (Plate 37, B). While the fact that a piece of furniture has round pins cut off flush with the surface does not in itself prove it to be new or fraudulent, we shall feel more comfortable about any intended purchase if it has irregularly shaped pins which project a bit—and incidentally if the piece is right in every other way.

THE MARKS OF SAWS

For thousands of years the inhabitants of wooded countries have sawed lumber with various adaptations of the pitsaw system. With this system the log was placed above a long narrow pit occupied by one of the sawyers, the other sawyer standing upon a platform built above the log. These two men worked back and forth between them a long narrow saw, and very slowly and painfully secured rough boards and timbers of something near the required sizes. In the earliest Pilgrim days, lumber was sawed by hand with pit saws. The first water-power sawmill is said to have been built at Piscataqua Falls, Maine, in 1634, and twenty years later many such mills were being operated by our New England streams.

Wind sawmills were built by the Dutch of Manhattan Island as early as 1633. The wonders of such a mill are recorded by an early writer who quaintly remarks, "One of them will do more work in an hour than fifty men in two days." All of these mills used the straight up-and-down or gash saw and, hence, the "kerf," or mark of the saw teeth, on any lumber sawed before 1850 will be practically straight and the marks running at right angles to the longitudinal grain of the wood (Plate 38, A). Some up-and-down or gash saws are still being operated in remote districts. Circular saws were first used in an experimental way about 1814 but were not common until after 1850. The teeth of the circular saw leave a very different kerf from that of the straight up-and-down saw. The circular saw, depending somewhat on its diameter and the speed with which the log is pushed against it, leaves on the surface of lumber, a curved kerf or mark of the rapidly revolving teeth (Plate 38, B). Early furniture frequently shows on hidden surfaces, such as the under side of table tops and the interior of cabinet pieces, the marks of saw teeth.

The only inference we can draw from these marks is this: even if furniture shows marks of the up-and-down saw, we cannot be sure that these marks mean great age, but we can be extremely sure that no genuine and intact piece of furniture made before 1815 will anywhere on its surfaces exhibit the curving marks of the teeth of the circular saw.

PLATE 38

A MARKS OF THE OLD UP-AND-DOWN OR GASH SAW ON UNDER SIDE OF A RED OAK FLOOR-BOARD OF ABOUT 1780

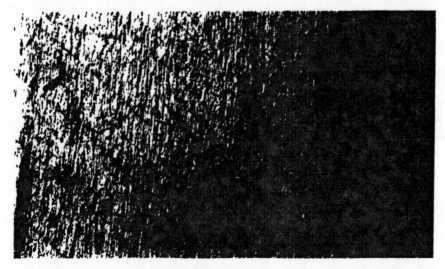

B MARKS OF THE CIRCULAR SAW, WHICH WAS ONLY UNCOMMONLY USED BEFORE THE MIDDLE OF THE NINETEENTH CENTURY

THE SHRINKAGE OF TURNINGS

The radial shrinkage of all woods is always less than the tangential shrinkage. The shrinkage from the pith of the tree through the annular rings toward the bark is less than in a line at right angles to the curve of these same annular rings. Thus, if a round turning be made from green or only partially seasoned wood, this turning, when thoroughly dry, becomes more or less ovoid in shape. Many turned parts of early furniture were intentionally made from unseasoned woods so that their subsequent shrinkage would bind other supplemental parts firmly in place. The posts of turned chairs will nearly always show under the calipers their ovoid character.

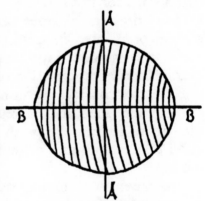

Fig. 21. The Shrinkage of Turnings

In our Fig. 21 may be seen the end section of an old and ovoid turning with the marks of the annular rings. The dimensions of the diameter B—B are greater because on this line the radial shrinkage has been less than on the line of the tangential shrinkage A—A.

While this shrinkage is not in itself an absolute proof of great age, turnings made from kiln-dried wood do not develop this tendency to become ovoid. The round turnings of factory reproductions made from thoroughly dried woods always remain round—they do not become ovoid with the passing of time. And if we were considering the purchase of a turned-post five-slat armchair, the fact that the posts were somewhat ovoid would be an argument toward its authenticity—and yet no one should purchase such a chair with ovoid posts if everything else about the chair is doubtful.

COMMENTS ON FRAUDS AND FRAUDULENT METHODS

As time goes on and the prices on antiques continually advance, the whole subject of fraudulent and "fake" furniture becomes of increasing importance and certainly of great moment to the amateur whose knowledge and experience do not qualify him to distinguish with certainty the genuine from the fraudulent.

If a piece is unfinished and "in the rough" we may much more easily judge it. In a genuine piece "in the rough" there is a consistency of color, both on the inner and outer surfaces, that speaks for itself. If any additions have been made, such as feet, drawers, or tops, and these additions have been stained or painted in attempted conformance with the old surfaces, these new parts may usually be located by careful examination and inspection of surfaces.

When we consider pieces that have been restored, cleaned off, and refinished, the amateur is likely to find it much more difficult to locate new parts, as all these processes tend to cover up any additions or repairs and to blend the new with the old.

The expert in examining refinished furniture can by a careful inspection find every addition or repair—but this ability is only acquired through years of experience, and I have found that this ability to tell the new from the old is usually found in someone whose experience has been gained in *personally dissecting and repairing old furniture.* There are old professional restorers and refinishers who have developed the power to such a point that they will merely give a casual glance at a refinished Windsor chair and remark, "Yes, nice chair, but it has one new leg and stretcher, and two new spindles"—and the opinion will be quite true. Any piece newly constructed entirely of old materials would be unworthy of even their comment unless it might possibly elicit a contemptuous grunt. These "old-timers" are probably our best judges as to authenticity and some collectors doubting their own knowledge will buy no important piece of furniture until its worth and genuineness has been verified by one of these men.

It has often been stated that the most gullible persons in furniture-collecting circles are the wealthy collectors who depend entirely on their own knowledge, and who, at the same time, have had no personal experience of any sort in dissecting, restoring, or working about old furniture.

The flair for discerning the genuine in old furniture does not exclusively dwell with the educated. I have seen this flair very well developed in ignorant and unlettered second-hand dealers. The mysterious manner in which some of these quite uneducated men can recognize beauty, age, and fineness, not only in furniture but in all sorts of ancient objects, is almost uncanny. They know antiques, not by periods, names, or dates, but by the objects' own beauty and worth and evidences of age.

There seems to be a widely extended feeling at present, particularly with the newer collectors, that there is hardly any genuine antique furniture available; that almost all the furniture shown in the antique shops is fraudulent and faked; that the country is full of stately old homes, the attics of which are crammed with fake pieces planted by dealers to be sold to the unsuspecting. In fact, some amateurs who have started to collect antique furniture become so nervous and frightened over the ever-present bogy of fakes that they hardly dare buy anything. Conditions do not warrant any such state of fear. It is quite true that there is plenty of faking and many fraudulent pieces are offered for sale. However, much of the dishonest work is so badly done and so very apparently new that it should deceive no one. It is strange but true that, having produced a fairly convincing fake, the faker seldom has the nerve to ask a price which would be right for a genuine piece. If an entirely original butterfly table is worth a thousand dollars, the faker places a price of two or three hundred dollars on his fraudulent butterfly, thereby proclaiming to the wise that something is wrong and that caution is necessary. We should very carefully scrutinize any pieces of the finer types of furniture which are offered to us at extremely low prices.

The location in which we find our furniture should in a manner influence our feeling about authenticity. If an old friend offers to sell us some of his family treasures, we are naturally not so very suspicious: while if we are delving in the stock of a dealer whose record is not too clean, we would examine with extreme care any possible purchase.

It is true that fraudulent furniture is sometimes "planted" in farmhouses and secondhand shops in the hope that the environment and the excitement of unexpected discovery will bring about a quick purchase without a thorough examination. It is also true that unscrupulous dealers will sometimes buy the contents of an old home in the country, and mix in with the genuine a few truckloads of trash and fakes. Thus the stage is set for an auction sale of the entire contents of the famous old so-and-so mansion. This method of crookedness does not usually work out well, because there are too many persons who know the details of the crooked plans. Gossip travels quickly by word of mouth and often by the time the auctioneer mounts his block the entire audience knows that it is attending what is known as a "phony auction."

To comment on the more agreeable side of the subject, there is still a very large quantity of antique furniture for sale in the shops which is quite genuine, authentic, and right in every way. It is simply a matter of becoming enough of an expert to distinguish the false from the true. The amateur must do the best he can with his available knowledge and not be heartbroken if he is occasionally "stung" with some piece that is not right. This *may* happen even to an experienced collector, but, if it does, he seldom says very much about the occurrence. It has been remarked that the usual procedure in such cases is to sell the offending piece in the evening to some less experienced and possibly myopic collecting friend; but this was probably the remark of some hardened and dyspeptic cynic.

FRAUDULENT FURNITURE MADE ENTIRELY OF NEW WOODS

It is quite a common occurrence to come across pieces of a valuable type, such as highboys, lowboys, butterfly tables, fine Windsor chairs, or desks, which have been made within the last twenty years. These pieces have sometimes been stained and painted, then cleaned off in exactly the same manner as if genuine. If such a piece has been but recently completed and has had no actual use, the lack of wear and the texture and color of the new wood both inside and out will usually loudly proclaim the truth. However, if the piece was a properly constructed maple lowboy made and treated twenty years ago and since subjected to the use and wear of a home, it is not always easy to judge its age. Butterfly tables have been much reproduced in the last twenty years and in some cases hard use has brought these reproductions to a very fair imitation of antiquity. I once had the experience of being offered in a home a pair of butterfly tables. They were frauds, rather well done but the offer of a pair of butterfly tables at eighty-five dollars each at once aroused my suspicions. Butterfly tables do not come to us often in pairs or flocks and at eighty-five dollars each. There are, these days, all sorts of good reproductions on the market, but made and sold *as reproductions* and with no intention to deceive. These reproductions are of course made of new wood, but every item of the old construction is followed. Mortice-and-tenon joints, pins, dovetails, and the stylistic details are fairly correct. Sometimes these pieces become in the hands of the unscrupulous the basis for dishonest work of various sorts. They may be scratched, marred, and pounded with different tools, then painted with a thin red cold-water paint. They may next be put out in the weather for a season, where the sun and rain will age them and bring a spurious appearance of antiquity. I have heard of one faker who buried new Windsor chairs in the deep muck of a swamp for a summer, thereby giving them quite a pleasing color of mellow age. I have heard of several fakers who, in specially constructed smokehouses, treated their new furniture to just the desired shade of brownness. However, the strong hamlike odor of furniture so treated should prevent our considering its purchase.

Very strong tea, coffee, and infusions of oak and butternut bark are sometimes used in the attempted changing of new woods into old. Strong lye mixed with mud is sometimes daubed over a piece of reproduction furniture and left for a time to burn and discolor it. It is probably true that the faker finds his best field in the smaller objects. It is much easier to produce a "fake" pipe box or stick-leg candlestand, than to bring forth a plausible six-leg highboy either of old or new woods. The candlestand is small and simple; while the highboy is complex, requiring all sorts of care about details of construction, wear on drawers and drawer runs, and, after all these are arranged, the faker must attempt to bring all the inner and outer surfaces to a smooth and uniform color and appearance of antiquity. Such faking may be, and is, attempted, but not with great success. We hear a great deal about the wonderful cleverness of furniture-fakers, yet it is my firm opinion that there is no faker living who can produce a fraudulent six-leg highboy that will for a moment deceive any one of our well-known American experts.

FRAUDULENT FURNITURE MADE ENTIRELY OF OLD WOODS

Many fakers in constructing their fraudulent furniture attempt to use only old woods, thereby thinking that the age of the material will conceal the fact that the pieces are newly constructed. I have seen many important pieces, such as fine tavern and butterfly tables, highboys and lowboys, Spanish-foot and Flemish-carved cane chairs, constructed entirely of old woods, sometimes worm-eaten.

These pieces are usually quite unconvincing. Even if old woods are used, they must be sawed, cut, and molded in the new work. When an old piece of wood is cut off, sawed, and planed, new surfaces are exposed and these fresh surfaces are very difficult to bring to any plausible appearance of age. Also, in attempting to produce an important piece of furniture, such as a highboy or chest, entirely of old materials, the faker has difficulty in finding a sufficient quantity of old clear material of a uniform color, thickness, and kind of wood. Thus, he may be forced to construct one drawer of thick tulipwood, and another drawer of thinner pine. The back may be partly of chestnut of dark color, partly of pine of light color. The old boards may show marks of brasses where no brasses should be or nail holes where no nail holes could possibly be required. One end, although of good wood, may show a reddish tint from old paints, while the opposite end although equally old, will be of a blackish cast. Dyes, stains, smoke, lye, mud, and dust may be used, but the piece is still usually a botch not at all convincing enough to confuse the expert. Such a piece will quite lack the delightful uniformity in color and texture of surfaces both inside and out which is the badge of authenticity worn by a genuine old piece.

The faker may attempt to satisfy his conscience by telling us that the piece is "all old" and so it may be, as to its materials, but not as to its time of manufacture.

Old and worm-eaten wood is often used in fraudulent furniture, but, when such a course is followed, the channels cut by the worms show all over the surface of the piece. When genuine old furniture is inhabited by worms, the only signs of their presence are the tiny round very sharp edge holes which are the front entrances of their homes. (Plate 39).

It is said that in Europe some of the most expert furniture-fakers keep trained organizations of worms which are turned loose in steel-lined rooms to work on whatever piece of fraudulent furniture requires their attention. There is an old and oft-repeated story that some American fakers produce wormholes by firing number ten shot at their completed work with a shotgun. This story is to be doubted, as such worm-holes would be splintered and rough and not at all like a genuine wormhole.

CHANGES IN GENUINE FURNITURE TO INCREASE ITS VALUE

Early furniture is changed in many illicit ways to better its type, add desirable features, and so increase its value.

Tavern tables with *plain stretchers* are furnished with square *turned stretchers* as the latter are more desirable. Tavern tables with *plain skirts* emerge from the faker's shop with *handsomely scrolled skirts*. Banister-back chairs go into the rear entrance carrying *simple crests*, later to appear on the sidewalk with handsome *heart-and-crown* or *carved crests*. *Plain rungs* of turned chairs are removed and *finely turned rungs* inserted in their place. The straight-edge boards of plain open-top cupboards are elaborately scrolled and the value of the piece greatly enhanced. Sunbursts and shells are carved on surfaces which originally bore no carving of any sort. Tremendous birds, presumably eagles, are carved on the front boards of the simple and common six-board chests, a position which as far as I know was never occupied on

PLATE 39

WORM-HOLES EXTERIOR AND INTERIOR OF WORM-EATEN WOOD

this type of genuine old American furniture by carved eagles or any other birds.

Plain but genuine old mahogany tables, chests of drawers, and sideboards are handsomely inlaid and such work if well done is very difficult to detect. Chests of drawers with plain feet after the ministrations of the faker will have ball-and-claw feet. Tops of highboys are fitted with four turned ball feet and a lower molding and become ball-foot chests.

Simple and original unturned tavern tables with square legs are taken apart, the legs placed in a lathe and handsomely turned. When such a table is re-assembled and the new turned surfaces carefully aged, it will pass in almost any company as genuine. And of course it really is an old and genuine table—except for some "improvements."

Simple lowboys which are in good condition except for the loss of the Dutch feet will often appear after a course of treatment with four entire new legs, displaying at the bottom fine Spanish or ball-and-claw feet. If these new legs are properly treated and colored this fraud is not too easy to discover, as every part of the lowboy with the exception of the four new legs, is original and right.

A small chest of drawers with feet removed may be placed upon a slightly larger chest of drawers, and a high and impressive chest-on-chest is the result.

Windsor chairs originally having a feeble bamboo-turned underbody are fitted with fine vase-turned legs, with turnings just a shade finer and more bulbous than were ever possessed by any genuine American Windsor.

The long back spindles and top bow of an ordinary low-back Windsor armchair are removed; new and longer spindles are inserted, and a new and longer top bow fitted into place. Thus an ordinary chair has been turned into a very impressive high-back Windsor armchair of a rare type.

The front cabriole legs and Dutch feet are removed from chairs of early Chippendale style, and carved legs with ball-

and-claw feet are substituted. On other chairs, large Spanish feet are substituted for the original turned feet.

Butterfly tables, being very valuable, are favorite objects for the efforts of the faker. Having found a small tavern table, preferably without any drawer, he re-cuts the boards of the skirt and the stretchers and transforms the tavern table into a table with legs raked in two directions; holes are bored in the centre of the side stretchers, to receive the lower ends of the wings made of old woods. A small drop-leaf top of old wood, carrying rusty butterfly hinges fastened with hand-wrought nails, is pinned in place and the "butter-fly" is ready for any painting, dyeing, or ageing processes the faker may have in view.

Such a butterfly table does not mislead the expert collector. To build and install a drop-leaf table top with its joints and hinges so that it will appear old is a difficult matter. New hinges, applied with old nails and rusted with salt and vinegar, are more rusty than any genuine old hinges. The under side of the drop leaves are unmarked by the tops of the wings and possibly the faker forgets to stain the upper edge of the wings under the leaves. The stretchers, instead of showing, as on genuine butterfly tables, only a slight wear under the lower ends of the wings, are worn evenly across.

INGENIOUS UTILIZATION OF OLD PARTS

I have seen many large tables of various types constructed around single odd highboy drawers carrying their original brasses. As the first thing any collector usually does when he examines such a piece is to pull open a drawer, an old drawer with old brasses gives a momentary impression of authenticity probably soon dispelled when various inaccuracies are discovered on both the inner and outer surfaces of the table. The drawer is quite all right, but everything else about the table is fraudulent.

An ingenuity and inventiveness worthy of a better cause is

shown by fakers in the utilization of old parts of small flax wheels, large wool wheels, and yarn reels. All of these three classes of objects are plentiful and cheap and have many finely turned parts. These handsome turnings are used to produce all sorts of "early" candlestands, footstools, and small benches. In the production of these smaller and uncomplex objects, the faker does his most convincing work. Therefore, if we purpose buying any of them in a finished condition, we should examine each piece with the greatest care. When these small objects are "in the rough," it is much more easy to form opinions as to their authenticity.

I think a sufficient number of examples of the dishonest and doubtful work of the furniture-faker have been mentioned, although this list is by no means complete.

The ingenious and unscrupulous are ever busy with all this sort of work, and it is remarkable that they cannot realize that such crookedness seldom brings prosperity. I have yet to see a confirmed furniture-faker who achieved any sort of permanent prosperity or one who was not in trouble most of the time with dissatisfied customers, suits at law, or the police. The antique dealers who become prosperous are those honest individuals who tell the exact truth about their goods, build up a satisfied clientèle, and deal in the finer pieces.

The poor furniture-faker at best leads a nervous and unhappy life. He has so many things to think of and so much trouble with his customers. Probably he often wonders in the long watches of the night whether the slippery path is the easier one.

While we do not excuse or condone the dark and devious doings of the faker, he, like other interesting criminals, bandits, bootleggers, and smugglers, adds a thrilling note of excitement and uncertainty to our prosaic lives. Does not each one of us get a virtuous glow over our own ability to discover a fraud and to be able to distinguish the false from the true? If there were no fakers, and hence no fraudulent furniture, I am sure we would find collecting much less interesting. The faker may very well be a hidden blessing as carefully disguised as one of his own lowboys.

Imagine a world of collectors with no frauds or fakes to uncover, and upon which to develop a proper collecting "edge."

INDEX

Printed in the United States
144197LV00004B/31/P

9 781444 603217

ML

5/oq